THE UNFINISHED REFORMATION

THE
UNFINISHED
REFORMATION

HANS ASMUSSEN

ERNST FINCKE

MAX LACKMANN

WOLFGANG LEHMANN

RICHARD BAUMANN

Translated by **ROBERT J. OLSEN**

Foreword to the English Edition by

JOHN P. DOLAN, C.S.C.

FIDES PUBLISHERS ASSOCIATION
NOTRE DAME, INDIANA

Translated from the German, KATHOLISCHE REFORMATION,
Schwabenverlag, Stuttgart, 1958.

Library of Congress Catalog Card Number: 61-10368

FOREWORD TO THE ENGLISH EDITION

by

JOHN P. DOLAN, C.S.C., Ph.D.*

The history of the Reformation and of the inner divisions that preceded it has not yet been written: It will not be written until we arrive at some final explanation of the event that has allowed millions to live Christian lives outside the framework of the Church. This is a tragedy and an enigma that defies simple explanation. "It could never be," wrote Cardinal Newman over a century ago, "that so large a portion of Christendom should have split off from the communion of Rome and kept up a protest for three hundred years for nothing. . . . All aberrations are founded on and have their life in some truth or other, and Protestantism, so widely spread, so long enduring, must have in it, and must be witness of a great truth or much truth." [1] It is in this perspective that we must approach this contribution of five Lutheran pastors. The precondition of ecumenical activity is a willingness to reopen the history of the Reformation—and to clear the atmosphere of the ac-

---

* In this foreword to the English edition of *Katholische Reformation* (published in Germany in 1958), Father Dolan, Professor of History, University of Notre Dame, gives historical background for the seven circular letters of the *Sammlung* and the discussion by the five Lutheran pastors who are the authors of this book. The sympathy with which he accepts the sincerity of their convictions is in itself a triumph of his own scholarship and the ecumenical spirit. (Ed. note.)

[1] *Apologia,* p. 188.

cumulated poison of bias and misconception that has continued to cloud both Catholic and Protestant historians.

Part of the difficulty in understanding the Reformation is technical. At no other period in the past have religious and political, economic and social factors been so closely interwoven. Even for the serious student this intricate interpenetration blurs the focus of objectivity. Furthermore the Reformation is not a closed chapter even in the sense that the Rennaisance, the Enlightenment and the French Revolution are closed chapters. What happened at Augsburg and Trent is as much an ingredient of twentieth century thought as it was of sixteenth century thought. Continuing division continues to color our present image of the Church; it conditions the whole approach to religion in the Western world. Yet the continuing impact which renders objectivity so difficult, makes it imperative that we do come to grips with the problem and uncover some final explanation of this enigma.

To achieve this we must attempt something more than a mere evaluation of Luther's personality. Nor is it sufficient merely to examine the immediate historical antecedents: the conditions in Luther's time which seemed to call for reform. The preliminary task is to examine the very notion of reform itself—a notion essentially Christian in its source and development.

There can be no doubt that the notion of reform is intimately interwoven with the Christian themes of spiritual rebirth, regeneration, and conversion. Baptism is regeneration; and renewal or reform of the inner man is the fulfillment of that baptismal regeneration. Particularly for St. Paul is this a central theme. In the letter to the Romans Paul warns his disciples not to be conformed to the world, but to be transformed or reformed in accordance with the

renovation of their minds.[2] Writing to the Colossians and
Corinthians, he portrays the renovation of the inner man
as a reformation in the image of God.[3] It is clear that for
the early Christians, religion was not merely a code of ethics
or an intellectual movement; it was above all, life itself,
which must continually reform or renew itself through
contact with Christ, the source of life.

This is the root concept of the liturgy with its insistence
on the repeated sacrifice of Christ as the life-giving center
of Christian reform. The antithesis of creation and reformation in the Incarnation is brought out very clearly in
the orations of the old Roman Christmas liturgy.[4] This
theme is even more frequently emphasized in the non-
Roman Western liturgies such as the Visigothic and the
Ambrosian. And today in the Offertory of the Roman Mass
we pray: "O God, who established the nature of man in
wondrous dignity and still more admirably reformed
it. . . ." The liturgical nexus between reform and evange-
lism is nowhere more apparent than in the prayer following the reading of the Gospel in the Mass: "By the words
of the Gospel, may our sins be taken away." The taking
away of sins through the word of God is a reform element
that Catholics share with Protestants.

The Fathers of the Church are at one in stressing continued reform as an intrinsic element in Christianity. Tertullian uses the term in the sense of a return to a previous
condition; yet in the reform symbol there is also the note of
a vital transcendence. In his treatise on the resurrection of
the dead he sees, in the recurrence and preservation of all

---

2 Romans 12:2.
3 R. C. Trench, *Synonyms of the New Testament* (Grand Rapids, Mich.,
1948), pp. 641 ff.
4 J. A. Jungmann, *Missarum Sollemnia* (Vienna, 1952), pp. 78 ff.

things in nature, a similarity to the resurrection of bodies.[5]
This is the renewal which goes beyond the previous condition. In his *Apologeticum* he stresses the fact that Christians
were to receive a "fuller grace" than the Jews had had.
This was to be brought about through reform and illumi-
nation by Christ.[6] The Pauline doctrine of the reform of
the divine image in man is synthesized by Hilary of Poitiers
in his *De Trinitate*. For Hilary the reform of man is a return to Paradise and the attainment of a much higher state.
And for St. Ambrose, also, reform implies spiritual progress. Hilary and Ambrose, along with St. Augustine, furnished the inspiration for the great Church reform of
Gregory VII, the authority of Hilary in particular enabling
reform to be defined as more than mere restoration.[7]

Among the Greek Fathers the reform motif is associated
with a deep eschatological element. The idea of restoration
and renewal is especially found in the Alexandrian theologians. Origen and Clement both stress the restoration of
creational integrity. For Origen, the final restoration, the
apocatastasis or eschatological re-establishment meant
man's restoration to the state which rational nature possessed when there was no need of eating from the tree of
knowledge of good and evil.[8]

Eusebius of course saw the restoration of the Roman
Empire as part of the reform of mankind; this restoration
was linked with the reformation of man through Christ.[9]
St. John Chrysostom's attempt to reform the urban society
of his day and his criticism of the unholy alliance of Church
dignitaries with the heirs of the Theodosian Empire re-

5 *De resurrectione mortuorum*, 6 f. Corp. Christ., Ser. Lat. II, 935.
6 *Apologeticum*, 21, 6.
7 G. Ladner, *The Idea of Reform* (Cambridge, 1959), p. 152.
8 *De Principiis III*, 6, 3, G.C.S.
9 *Historia Ecclesiastica X*, 456 ff.

sulted in his own death. But though his practical reform attempt failed, the ideas he applied to Christendom as a whole were to reappear and to be reapplied by St. Augustine. Those ideas expressed in Augustine's clerical and monastic reform ideology have influenced every corporate reform movement since then.

By the time of Augustine, reform movements had shifted from the early individualistic emphasis on renewal and improvement to a more institutional and sociological emphasis. Augustine's stress is on the communal nature of the Church. This communal mindedness must of course be understood in terms of the conditions of the time. During Augustine's own lifetime, the Emperor Theodosius had declared Christianity the officially recognized religion of the realm. It had become the cornerstone of law and order; conformity with its faith and discipline was a political requirement. Yet the justification of the authority of the institutional Church must be seen in the context of the Church as a community of love within this objective political-religious order. For Augustine the Church is "a congregation of men in which brotherly love is at work." [10] In this way the Church had a Christocentric dimension of faith and hope that set it apart from the temporal destinies of Greece and Rome.

In the *City of God* the sociological emphasis deepens, since the communion of saints now has the framework of the Roman *civitas* or *res publica*. Yet even here the notion of "Church reform" has not yet appeared. For Augustine "Church reform" is individual reform: the *ecclesia sine macula et ruga* [11] continues to exist in spite of the imperfections of its members. Yet this failure to discuss the

10 *De Fide et symb.* 9, 21.
11 Ephesians 5:27.

notion of institutional reform is hardly surprising. It was not until the sixteenth century that a concentrated effort was made to define the Church in theological terminology. The Christian life of the early Middle Ages was so much a part of the Church itself that a specific ecclesiology hardly seemed necessary. The first explicit treatment of the Church in this fashion—the *De Regimine Christiana* of James of Viterbo—appeared only in the thirteenth century.

Nevertheless it is true that the Augustinian notion of the Church as the City of God furnished the ground for the temporal dominance of Rome in Western Europe. Yet as the Church became more closely integrated into the feudal system, the institutional aspect of the Church came more and more into the foreground. Of particular importance is the fact that monasticism, after Cluny, was absorbed by the Church as one of its integral parts. The monks became the bearers of religious culture within the ecclesiastical-clerical institution; they became the institutors of the notion of ecclesiastical reform.

Although historians now deny the overriding role of Cluny in the reform of the Church in the eleventh and twelfth centuries and limit its influence to the monastic area,[12] nevertheless Cluny did reaffirm the scriptural reform ideas of the Fathers.[13] Emphasis was laid upon the fact that the reform of sinful humanity lay in the monastic ideal of achieving a return to a truly Christian life by the renunciation of terrestrial joys.

This was a far cry from the vast plan of religious reform and social reconstruction which Tellenbach terms the

[12] A. Fliche, *La Reform grégorienne* (Louvain, 1925), p. 174.
[13] G. Tellenbach, *Church-State and Christian Society* (Oxford, 1959), p. IX.

Gregorian Revolution and which many regard as the turning point of medieval civilization. Yet the monastic reform ideal did play a large role in this "revolution." The latest historian of the Gregorian Reform, N. E. Cantor, points out that it was the logical but unfortunate outcome of the equilibrium between the *imperium* and the *sacerdotium* which had developed from the time of Charlemagne. As the Church in the late tenth and eleventh centuries penetrated more and more into the world, imposing all its ideals on society, it began to face the dangerous possibility of losing its distinctive identity and hence its leadership.[14]

The increase in lay piety created a new problem for the Church with its traditional hierocratic ideal. The danger was that the Church might become completely absorbed by the Christianized *mundus*. The eremetic and ascetic movements resulting from the formation of the reformed monastic organizations—Carthusians, Cistercians and others—were the first reaction to this situation. Their reform ideal was the return to pristine poverty and the spiritual tone of the apostolic Church. It was logical enough to attempt to carry this reform to the entire Church and then to the entire world. The origin of Gregory VII's radical attack on the whole prevailing Christian order can be traced to this conviction. St. Romuald, founder of the Italian eremetic movement, wanted to turn the entire world into a vast hermitage. A total disregard for the sanction of social custom, the substitution of unbridled zeal for wisdom and moderation wrought havoc even with the institution of monasticism itself. This recklessness destroyed for the most part the very penetration of the mo-

[14] H. E. Cantor, "The Crisis of Western Monasticism," *American Journal of History*, LXV, p. 61.

nastic ideal into civil society. What did emerge however
was the fact that the ascetic ideal alone would hardly
suffice.

"The great movement of reform aimed, and partly succeeded in monachizing the Church by putting before the
clergy and even the laity, monastic discipline and monastic
practices and ideals as the universal way of salvation." [15]
Instead of the identification of the world and the Church,
the twelfth and thirteenth centuries were marked by a
growing separation between the two. The loss of prestige
by the monks would still be echoed centuries later in Eras-
mus's phrase, "Monachatus non est pietas," and in the
scorn and hatred that the institution evoked in Luther and
others.[16]

And there was the further difficulty that the ideal of
withdrawal could not be reconciled with the conception
of monarchical control and the subjection of lay society.
For the Gregorian reform was a struggle for right order
in the world. The basis of the reform was the assumption
that once the idea of a united Christendom was realized,
then its supreme ruler could only be the head of the
Church on earth.

Nevertheless it must be noted that the investiture struggle, along with the missionary journeys of St. Paul and the
Edict of Milan is one of the few notable steps in the long
process by which the Christian religion has endeavored to
lead the world to a complete acceptance of the reform
motive of the Gospels. It is of particular interest in our
own day when it seems to many that the root cause of our

[15] David Knowles, in *Bulletin of the John Knowles Library*, XXXIX,
132-33.

[16] "So oft er von der Moncherei redet, stroemt sein Herz über von Zorn
und Bitterkeit." Fr. Heiler, *Luthers Bedeutung fuer die christlich Kirche
in Luther in oekumenischer Sicht*, p. 169.

ills is the very incompleteness of the reform process. There is painful force in the contention that a new reforming step forward is needed if society is to be restored—and if the "plebs sancta" of the liturgy is to be realized.

The poverty movement, perhaps the most profound reform movement of the Middle Ages, was in a sense the final attempt of the medieval religious spirit to reform the world. At the same time that Bernard of Clairvaux strove to impose his ideal of poverty on Church and society, Arnold of Brescia began a movement of reform that attacked the very possession of temporal goods by the Church. Although Arnold, as well as Peter Waldo and Joachim of Floris, was a heresiarch, the popularity of their cause nevertheless demonstrated a growing discontent with the institutionalized Church edifice. The poverty movement flowed in two directions, the leftist affecting practically all the medieval heresies from Joachim of Floris to John Huss, and the mendicant wing led by St. Francis and St. Dominic resulting in a greater centralization of papal authority through the agency of the friars.

Yet the endorsement of the mendicants and their grant of exemption by the papacy were to lead to the tension between the friars and the secular clergy which played such a predominant role in the breakdown of religious unity in the fifteenth and sixteenth centuries. Even after many centuries some question the feasibility of the absolute renunciation of worldly goods as a means of personal sanctification or reform. Lord Acton remarks: "Observe the degeneration of the principle of poverty in an altered society in the friars who followed the monks. It had enriched the old world and it impoverished the modern. For the Benedictines, the real inheritors of the old monastic and ascetic spirit, growing with the growth of Christendom, became wealthy and politically powerful. But the Franciscans, continuing to live on alms instead of giving them, multiplied overmuch." [17] Forming a sort of elite corps under the direction of the papacy, the mendicants also marked the culmination of the super-political unity that was so much the ideal of medieval Christianity. Yet the move came too late in reforming the Church. As the historian Christopher Dawson remarks, ". . . the prophetic and evangelical vocation of the early friars became subordinated to the demands of ecclesiastical power politics, and this produced a rift in the reforming movement from which medieval Christendom never recovered. . . . Henceforward during the later Middle Ages the reformers were pre-dominantly anti-Papal in spirit, as were the Spiritual Franciscans and Wycliffe, or supporters of the secular power like William of Ockham and Marsiglio of Padua." [18]

The apparent triumph of the Church in the investiture strife, which marked the so-called secularization of the medieval Church, was given a counterbalance by the addition of a mystical interpretation to the gigantic legal and economic structure of the Church militant. The expression "Mystical Body," which originally had a liturgical or sacramental meaning, took on a social connotation, applied to the Church's institutional and ecclesiological aspects. This transfer of a liturgical idiom to a juridical theme added a spiritual exaltation. Yet the juridical process continued unabated in bringing about what the late Cardinal Suhard terms "the replacing of the body of Christ by a corpse of the Church." [19] Nevertheless the *ens politicum* which was so much the application of Au-

[17] Abbot Gasquet, *Lord Acton and His Circle* (New York, 1906), p. 239.
[18] Christopher Dawson, *Religion and the Rise of Western Culture* (New York, 1950), p. 216.
[19] Cardinal Suhard, *Growth or Decline* (Fides, 1948), p. 28.

gustinian and Aristotelian categories to the Church in the peculiar historical setting of a feudalized society did not go unchallenged. The complaint of Dante that there were no theologians in Rome can in part be explained by the fact that most medieval popes were lawyers, identifying reform with a reshaping of the superstructure rather than the inner vitality of the Church. It is interesting to note that the Lateran Council of 1517 reissued the Bull *Unam Sanctam* on the very eve of those events which were the culmination of protests against the institutional aspects of the Church.

Perhaps one of the greatest difficulties in evaluating the impact of the reform ideal in the late medieval and modern periods lies in the fact that the ideal has often identified itself with the substrata of the intellectual growth of the time. The undercurrents of history, the dynamism that shaped both the political and sociological structure of modern Western civilization, have been too often missed by the critical schools in their quest for minutiae and in their avoidance of generalizations. Two strong currents emerged as the medieval synthesis disintegrated, both of which played an important part in the reform movement: the notion of progress and the theology of nominalism.

Progress, or the new evaluation of time, influenced by Averroism, became one of the most powerful agencies whereby Western thought at the end of the Middle Ages was transformed and energized. The optimistic philosophy of progress flowing from an appraisal of man's relation to time stirred the entire thirteenth century. Time, hitherto equivalent with transitoriness and signifying the frailty of the present world, became a factor in the notion of reform. The rejection of the Augustinian dualism of time and eternity produced a secularization of the Christian concept of continuity. A new approach to life was reflected in a dialectical shift from time's fragility to its ever-flowing dynamism. Thus the Church, as a juridical body, became for many a frozen entity as superfluous as it had been in the fourth and fifth centuries. The choice between the incarnational view that the world sanctified by the blood of the God-Man is more than a vale of tears and the eschatological view of the transcendence of religion, making life little more than a pilgrimage to God, became more and more acute.

In the fourteenth century the nominalism of William of Ockham became the vehicle of an incipient idea of progress. Nominalism as a decisive element of reform has for the most part been neglected by historians. Any attempt to evaluate it merely in the terms of its logical or metaphysical aspects overlooks the all-important fact that it was fundamentally a theological awakening. Unfortunately, philosophers, in an attempt to question its departure from high scholasticism and to judge it by comparison with certain forms of thirteenth century Aristotelianism, have underestimated it as an intellectual force vitally formative in Western religious thought. Their oversight is not unlike that of those who endeavor to understand the sixteenth century reformation in terms of the decrees of Trent or the Catholic restoration.

The late Middle Ages, laboring under the burden of an over-institutionalized Church, which was but one aspect of the intense corporate consciousness of the time, sought in the spiritual realm something that would offer greater immediacy with the divine. Nominalism was one answer to this quest. It is evident in the Rhenish mystics, Eckhart, Suso and Tauler, in their senses of "God within." Wycliffe, Huss, and Biel color it with Platonic realism.

Gerson and D'Ailly inject it in their notion of the universal Church. It is above all reflected in the popular piety of the time. The multiplicity of Masses for the dead, the accumulation of relics, the laicism of the *Devotio Moderna* are expressions of this seeking for a contact with God outside the established framework of a departmentalized Church. The movement which Inhart de la Tour terms "Evangelisme," [20] the emphasis on Pauline rather than scholastic theology so much in evidence on the eve of the Reformation, is but a further development of this mentality. The emphasis on Mariology and the preoccupation of the fourteenth and fifteenth century theologians with predestination can at least in part be traced to a strong current of nominalism that carried seeds of reform rejecting institutionalized religion in favor of more dynamic force.[21]

The incessant pleadings of those two great personages of the Avignon period, Catherine of Sienna and Brigit of Sweden, place the importance of Church reform on the same level with the return of the popes to Rome. Nor were individuals alone the advocates of reform during this period; the general councils of the Middle Ages were inspired for the most part by reform needs. From the first Lateran Council (1139) until the acknowledged reform councils of the fifteenth century, the theme ran through most of the legislation enacted. The episcopal *Gravamina* of the Council of Vienne (1317) contain almost all of the abuses that were to come up for discussion in the century before the Reformation.

The reform ideas of the medieval period must, of course,

20 Inhart de la Tour, *Le Origines de la Reform,* III, "L'Evangelisime" (Paris, 1948).

21 Bergson, *Les Deux Sources de la morale et de la Religion* (Paris, 1948), pp. 22 ff.

be considered in the light of the historical conception of the Church at that time. For the Church had become so closely integrated into the feudal order that its institutional aspects were pushed more and more into the foreground.

During the last two centuries that preceded the Protestant Reformation, the call for reform, for a return to the primitive form of Christianity which had its roots in the very nature of revelation and whose lineaments had been stamped on it by the early Church, became even louder. This call originated in the consciousnesss that Christ's foundation as historically realized in its individual members no longer corresponded to the ideal; in other words, that it was not what it should be. In this respect reform was no new thing but as old as the Church itself.

Although for a time the institution of papal supremacy was not attacked, the demand for reform was gradually aimed at the worldliness of the Church's hierarchy and particularly at the centralization of authority in the Roman Curia. The situation created by the Western Schism brought together an alliance of the conciliar theory and the demand for reform that was so detrimental to the Church in the late Middle Ages. Effective reform could be achieved only by a limitation of papal authority by a general council. The aim of the conciliarists was to heal the schism by a *reformatio in capite,* which meant a curtailing of the powers of papal government. It was to be a return to ancient law. Dietrich von Niem was but one of many sincere Catholics who, though attacking the Roman Curia and advocating a circumscribing of its power, nevertheless felt that a reform could be accomplished by regularly convened councils. Yet, though a union was achieved at Constance, the reform, much to the dismay of the ultramontane Catholics, was again delayed. There remained, however, a conviction that reform would come: "At no time was the Church of the Middle Ages unconscious of the fact that interior recollection, penance, a return to the ancient ideals of the priestly and monastic life were the core of any reform." [22] The increase of curial abuses during the Renaissance, the extension of papal taxes, the sale of important ecclesiastical offices only enkindled a stronger desire for the reform of Church officialdom.

A century later the Fifth Council of the Lateran, returning to the pattern of the papal councils of the Middle Ages, struggled with the question of whether it could command sufficient courage and determination to undertake a serious reform of the Church. "Men must be changed by holiness, holiness must be altered by men" were the words addressed by Aegidius of Viterbo in his sermon at the opening of the Council. The demand that "judgment must begin in the house of the Lord" was unheeded. The Lateran synods of the Middle Ages could not be revived in an altered world. The Council terminated in March of 1517. In October of that same year Martin Luther nailed his ninety-five theses to the door of the court-church of Wittenburg and the flood that was to destroy Church unity for the next 400 years was loosed.

The preliminary condition for an effective movement towards reform was the presence of a new spirit, not only at the center, but also the periphery of the Church. Regulations and measures can only lead to reform if they are enforced and complied with. Ideas and ideals demand internal assent and enunciation by those who are prepared to uphold them at the cost of personal sacrifice. There

22 H. Jedin, *Geschichte des Konzils von Trient* (Freiburg, 1950), I, p. 23.

was little enough of this spirit in the ranks of hierarchy or any other estate of the Church.

"The Protestant Reformation owed its success to the fact that the Catholic attempts at reform which sprouted from the soil of the Church did not come to maturity." [23]

Although it may be somewhat of an exaggeration to identify the Reformation with the personality of Luther and to equate Protestantism with his doctrines, nevertheless from an ecumenical point of view we must accept the statement of Sell: "das Prinzip des Protestantismus im Grunde die Person Martin Luther ist." [24] There is scarcely a single instance in history in which one individual has such significance in a tremendous historic upheaval as Martin Luther assumes in the Reformation. To consider him merely as the enunciator of ideas traceable to a number of early theologians or to maintain, as Heller does, that his contribution to the Reformation was small (that it was, as it were, the spark that ignited the powder and that he was an occasion, not a cause, of the Reformation), is a view that no serious student of the period now accepts.

It must be borne in mind that the Reformation is not merely an historical event, a thing that happened in the past. It is an event still going on. One must realize that it is an extraordinarily complicated fact, in itself as well as in its centuries-old structure. It is as much a social movement as it is the work of outstanding individuals. If history is an uninterrupted welling up of life in a multitude of divisions, currents, and countercurrents, formed by changing influences and varied impulses, then, like life itself, it is basically a mystery. The necessity of going be-

[23] "Die protestantishe Reformation konnte ihre Erfalge nur deshalb erringen, veil die katholischen auf dem Boden der Kirche sprossenden Reform bestrebungen, ihr Zeil nicht erreicht hatten." Jedin, *op. cit.,* p. 123.

[24] *Katholizismus und Protestantismus* (Leipzig, 1908), p. 40.

yond a merely dogmatic evaluation of the event must be
stressed if we are to have a historical understanding of the
Reformation. A dispassionate consideration of the event
must not only have the quality of objective inquiry, it
must free itself of that destructive force of self-interest
that inevitably leads to fruitless controversy. The Reformation must be fit somehow into the divine plan of salvation. We must be convinced of the possibility that in a
non-Catholic religious movement, in accordance with the
human spirit, and hence in accordance with God's will,
real religious Christian values can be found.

Unfortunately this attitude has not been that of Catholics regarding this Reformation. Beginning with the first
Catholic biographer of Luther, his contemporary, John
Cochlaeus, there has been a four-century old attempt to
portray Luther as the frightful destroyer of the Church,
a person who was motivated only out of envy of Tetzel
and hatred for the abuse of Indulgences, a hypocrite and
a false monk. The legends relating to Luther's Slavic
(Hussite) origin, his affair with Catharina von Bora, and
the circumstances of his death, which Catholics have kept
alive for centuries, can be traced to the writings of this
impassioned man.[25]

This attempt to paint Luther in the darkest hues, by
taking his remarks out of context and appraising him in
terms of such matters as his broken vows and his approval
of Philip of Hesse's bigamy, continued throughout the
following century, fostered by elements of confessional
absolutism and the rationalism of the Enlightenment.
One of the few Catholic attempts to evaluate Luther and
the reforms in terms of historical objectivity was con-

---

[25] *Joannis Cochlaei de actis et scriptis Martini Lutheri . . . fideliter con-
scripta* (Moguntia, 1549).

demned and put on the Index. The work of Louis Maim-
bourg, *Histoire du Lutheranisme,* published in 1680, was
a sincere effort to dispel some of the malicious legends
concerning Luther that were the heritage of the seventeenth century. Yet the *rabies theologorum* was still alive
enough to result in the author's expulsion from the Society of Jesus.

Bossuet, inspired with a sincere desire to achieve
Christian reunion, an inspiration which he shared with
Leibnitz,[26] wrote his famous *Histoire des Variations des
églises protestantes,* in 1688.[27] Basically an attempt to lead
the various confessions back to the Catholic fold by dem-
onstrating the falsity of their doctrines in their continual
variations, it was to influence Catholic evaluation of
Luther even to our own time. The work was primarily
that of a theologian and its historical value is hindered by
the lack of primary sources. To Bossuet, the basic error
of Protestantism was its failure to comprehend the true
nature of the Church and it thus remains "un amas de
sectes divisées entre elles qui se frappent d'Anatheme les
unes les autres." [28]

The Protestant picture of Luther, as Zeeden points out,
underwent a similar distortion.[29] The late sixteenth century
had already begun to regard him not merely as a personality,
but as the central figure in the theological-historical development of the world. Luther became fixed to a dogma.
Where Luther had restricted his doctrine of "true Christianity" to his interpretation of the Scriptures, his successors
restricted it to the teachings of Luther, thus destroying

[26] F. X. Kiefl, *Leibnitz und die religioese Wiedereinigung Deutschlands*
(1925), pp. 40 ff.
[27] Bossuet, *Oeuvres* (Paris, 1743), Vol. III.
[28] *Ibid.*
[29] E. Zeeden, *Martin Luther und die Reformation* (Frieburg, 1950).

that freedom of conscience which was so much the original doctrine of their founder. Luther was transported
to a position where one no longer evaluates but adores—
"into the sanctum and the mystery of God." No longer did
his followers draw from the same well as the reformer;
instead they received water only from his hands. The very
personality of Luther changed with the changes of Protestantism. Luther had proceeded from a deeply personal
experience of faith; his successors transformed this into a
principle, or rather principles, which were binding upon
their followers. "A living experience became a dogmatic
theology. Luther soon vanished behind his work. He became a myth." He who had been during his lifetime a
great genius fighting against the abuses of the Church had
within two generations become a Father of the Church,
venerated as the founder of religion. He ceased to be a
man and became instead a compendium of truth and orthodoxy.

The Pietists of the seventeenth century, with their
spirit of religious revivalism, found in Luther a model for
their call to a deeper spiritual life, a lessened emphasis on
controversial dogma and ritual, and a wider practice of
the Christian virtues. Both Spener and Francke represented a return to Luther's zeal for popular education
and an extension of his philanthropic efforts. Their endeavor exposed Luther's doctrines for the first time to the
investigations of secular historians. Arnold, in his interpretation (*Historia Lutheranismi,* 1692), turns once again
to the personality of Luther, to a study of his inner spiritual development.

Yet the writers of the Enlightenment tended to evaluate
Luther in terms of his medieval background. For Fred-
erick the Great he was an "enraged monk" and a

"barbarian writer." The rationalistic theologians of the eighteenth century continued to ascribe Luther's greatness to the fact that he liberated Christians from the fetters of episcopal suppression and made freedom the possession of every believer. For Goethe the Reformation was "eine Quark"—mere nonsense, in which the personality of Luther alone was of any real value or interest. Fichte, in his first address to the German nation in 1807, praised Luther as a national leader but found his teachings quite uninteresting.

Nowhere is the mediocrity of Catholic scholarship in this country more in evidence than in the lack of real interest in the work that has been accomplished in recent decades by German Catholic historians in the field of Reformation studies. It is a shame that so few American Catholic historians have interested themselves in this all important field of history. This, after all, is a country where the vestiges of the Reformation are far more in evidence than in the nation of their origin. The interest in interfaith movements, so much a part of the American scene, is too often upset by a naiveté in which the reform of the sixteenth century is viewed as the work of renegade monks, a phase of history that can be dismissed with the anathemas of Trent—or disposed of with a few disparaging clichés. Yet it is a truism that the wound in Christendom can be healed only after a penetrating reappraisal of its historical causes. No ecumenical movement can survive if it separates itself from the *traditio historica* of the Church.

A rebirth of Reformation studies found its antecedents in the very beginnings of critical historical studies. It is a phenomenon that can be traced to the movement in German universities that made the last century the great period of scientific history. Throwing off the shackles of the

Enlightenment and dispelling the mists of Romanticism, the German Catholics of the early nineteenth century are to be thanked for initiating critical research in the Reformation field at a time when the consciousness of the role they were to play in a unified Germany was in its infancy.

The publication of Möhler's *Symbolik* in 1832 and of the *Reformation* of Döllinger in 1846-48 are milestones in the breakthrough that was to bring to German Catholic historians and, through them, to the historians of other countries a consciousness of the position of the Church in its true historical perspective. Writing of Döllinger Lord Acton says: "If history cannot confer faith or virtue, it can clear away the misconceptions and misunderstandings that turn men against one another. . . . He learnt to think more favorably of the religious influence of Protestantism, and of its efficacy in the defence of Christianity; but he thought as before of the spiritual consequences of Lutheranism proper. When people said of Luther that he does not come well out of his matrimonial advice to certain potentates, to Henry and to Philip, of his exhortations to exterminate the revolted peasantry, of his passage from a confessor of toleration to a teacher of intolerance, he would not have the most powerful conductor of religion that Christianity has produced in eighteen centuries condemned for two pages in a hundred volumes." [30]

Even after the exhaustive work that followed the opening of the Vatican archives by Leo XIII, the works of these two men can be read today as remarkable insights into the Reformation and pre-Reformation periods. Although Döllinger followed Ranke in believing that the papacy was an institution that outlived its historical context (a belief that the resurgence of the papacy forty years later

[30] *History of Freedom and Other Essays.*

was to utterly refute), he must be listed along with
Möhler as one of the most distinguished scholars of
nineteenth century Germany. It is a great tragedy that
Döllinger, who contributed as perhaps no other Catholic
to the development of historical research, who attracted to
his person scholars not only from Germany, but from Eng-
land (Lord Acton) and France as well, should have broken
with the Church during the Vatican Council. His defec-
tion not only bore in its wake many of the most promising
historians of the period—Moriz, Ritter, and Druffel, to
name three—but it impaired Catholic research for generations to follow. The continuity of a strong Catholic interest in the Reformation and the production of outstanding
scholars were, however, not entirely impeded.

The next generation of German scholars were to develop in the atmosphere of the *Klein deutch* and the *Kulturkampf,* conditions that could not help but color and
weaken the objectivity of their writings. Janssen's influence
by both Döllinger and Möhler, the aim to produce "eine
bunte Mappe aus dem Zeitalter der Reformation" cannot
be overlooked, but it was rather an avowed attempt to
emancipate himself from the confines of confessionalism
and the vestiges of the Enlightenment that, in his own
words, was the aim of his research. Although he was no
member of the Klein deutch party in the German question
of the day, his enthusiasm for a unified Germany colored
his works. His *History of the German People,* granted its
popularity was in no small part due to its dramatic appearance in the midst of the Kulturkampf, was nevertheless one
of the most important writings in the last century on the
Reformation period. Yet even his Catholic readers were
aware of its apologetical tone and the over-rosy picture he
painted of Church deficiencies in the fifteenth century.

Nonetheless his work gave an impulse to research into the
conditions within the Church on the eve of the Reformation and inspired writers like Laemer, Falk, and Paulus.
That the Germans were the scholars to explore an entirely
new field of research in the newly opened Vatican archives [31] and that Catholics were in the forefront in this
epoch-making work, can be credited to men like Möhler
and Döllinger. The latter's work was carried on by his fa-
vorite student, Ludwig von Pastor, already risen to fame
through the publication of the first volume in his *History
of the Popes*. Both student and teacher were Catholic in
mind and heart. In Janssen, the spirit of the newly united
Germany, the priest, and the apologist might be contrasted
with Pastor, the Rhinelander, to whom the lecture halls of
the universities had been closed by the government. In
both, the element of polemics is found, but in Pastor there
is evidence of the laymen's independence from theology
and ecclesiastical direction.

The turn of the century—the era of Bulow, of the Center
Party, of the reconciliation of the Catholic party in politics
—witnessed a continuation of Catholic Reformation research. The appearance in 1903 of Denifle's *Luther und
Luthertum* enkindled a fire that has not yet burned itself
out. If Denifle opened up the field of study of late medieval
mysticism and the early development of Luther and his
relation to scholasticism, he nevertheless left his readers,
Catholic as well as Protestant, with a strong taste of bias
and attack. The steadfast Dominican was attacking the

31 The *Koeniglich Preussische Historische Station* founded in Rome in
1888 and the *Quellen und Forschungen aus Italienischen Archiven und
Bibliotheken,* although under Protestant leadership, attracted prominent
Catholic scholars, Cardauns in particular. Anton de Wall as well as Hergen-
roether were influential throughout their friendship with the brother of
Louis XIII, Cardinal Giuseppe Pecci, in his decision to open the archives.

fallen Augustinian with all the *studio et ira* that could be mustered. The appearance five years later of the Jesuit Grisar's three volumes on Luther, did much to mitigate the vitriolic attack of Denifle; the latter's work remains today in the eyes of both Catholic and Protestant scholars a poor picture of Luther and a work that can hardly be termed objective or biographical. Lortz's *Die Reformation in Deutschland* is far more acceptable to Catholic and Protestant alike.

The turning point in Catholic Reformation research, the shaking of its political attitude, and its emancipation from the defensive mentality that hindered the work of the previous decades was marked by the appearance in the academic world of the Rhineland scholar, Joseph Greving (1868-1919). The founding of the *Reformationsgeschichtlichen Studien und Texte* in 1905 by this professor of Church history at the University of Bonn filled a need that had long been felt by Germany's leading scholars. Fink, working in the late medieval and conciliar period; Paulus, authority on the Catholic resistance and the indulgence question; Pastor and Ehses, specializing in the Catholic reform and the Council of Trent; all unanimously voiced the need of a central organ of Catholic scholarship in Reformation studies. It was due to the untiring efforts of this Aachen-born priest that the dream was realized. Now in its fifty-fifth year and having withstood the vicissitudes of two world wars, this series of scholarly works embraces every aspect of the Reformation and pre-Reformation period which the objective scrutiny of source materials can produce. Its growing list of eighty-five volumes paints a graphic picture of this period culled from the lives of its bishops, its writers, its theologians, the movements that affected them and their imprint on the Church of that century.

Under the sponsorship of *Goerresgesellschaft* and with the same aim, the *Corpus Catholicorum* came to life in Munster in 1919. The original writings of Catholic scholars during the period of the reform has now risen to twenty-eight volumes. No study of the period can be complete without a knowledge of their scholarly contents. Cochlaeus, Eck, John Faber, Bishop Fisher are but a few of the writers presented. Now, under the brilliant editorship of Professor Hubert Jedin, the hopes and the tireless efforts of generations of Catholic scholars following their labors in *veritate et caritate* have culminated in a series of publications that is indispensable for any true view of the Reformation.

Writing in the *Historisches Jahrbuch* in 1955,[32] Jedin remarks that the history of the inner predispositions of the breakdown of the faith and the consciousness of this fissure has not yet been written. It can be written only when the atmosphere surrounding it has been disinfected. It is the great work of modern-day German scholarship that the atmosphere surrounding this period is being cleared of bias and prejudice, and it is a hope that Catholics everywhere will realize that the torn Christendom of today needs a *Traditio historica* as well as a *philosophia perennis*. In no other branch of history is the living element so in evidence as in this field; in no other is the religious and the political more closely entwined. Yet, too often its students have been lacking in objectivity because from the Protestant side all reform is traced to Luther, and from the Catholic viewpoint all has been evaluated in the light of Tridentine

[32] H. Jedin, "Fragen um Hermann von Wied," *Hist. Jahrbuch 74* (1955), s. 609.

decrees. It has been men like Jedin, Zeeden, Lortz, and Franzen who have dispelled much of the prejudice surrounding the Reformation and have carried on the century old tradition of an objective evaluation of this important epoch. It is only in the light of objectivity that this period can be properly understood and progress can be made toward a mending of the rent in the seamless robe of Christendom.

The idea of reform, then, runs through the entire history of Christianity. It is something more than a mere response to change or return to the dead past. It is defined as "the idea of freedom, intentional and ever perfectible, multiple, prolonged, and ever repeated effort by man to reassert and augment values pre-existent in the spiritual-material compound of the world." [33] Even to those who looked upon the Reformation of the sixteenth century as a unique and final collective reform, it was apparent that it was becoming necessary to reform the Reformation itself. "Now once again by all concurrence of signs, and by the general instinct of holy and devout men . . . God is decreeing to begin some new and great period in His Church, even to the reforming of reformation itself." [34]

Society today is going through what Cardinal Suhard termed a structural reform, a reform which is breaking the continuity of traditions and questioning consecrated values. And the Church is experiencing what Newman calls a succession of seasons, autumns and springs. As the permanent Incarnation of the Savior, it is not merely a juridical organization but it is also the Mystical Body of Christ. An overstressing of the external, institutional elements led to the rift in Christendom and yet a complete rejection of

---

[33] G. Ladner, *The Idea of Reform* (Cambridge, 1959), p. 35.
[34] Milton, *Areopagetica*, 32.

its visible organization, its hierarchy and sacraments, has made those outside its framework more and more conscious of the need to return to it. The pressing demand for reform in our day cannot be met by a mere return to the Reformation of the sixteenth century. It must be a reformation of the Reformation, a transformation. And this reshaping, this configuration of the old Reformation can take place only through a return to the universal, the ecumenical, the Catholic Church.[35]

The breakdown of Christian unity in the sixteenth century was above all a division in faith: yet the separation was of necessity preceeded by a breakdown of charity, and as long as charity founded on truth does not motivate and inspire, no ecumenical movement will succeed. Nowhere are the words of Augustine more applicable to reform than when he states that "the more we progress in His knowledge and charity, the more shall we become like to Him." Christianity is both truth and love.

[35] "Die heute notwendige Reformation kann darum nicht eine blosse Rükkehr zur Reformation des sechzehnten Jahrhunderts sein, sie muss vielmehr zugleich, um mit Wilfried Monod zu reden, eine, Reformation de Reformation, eine, Transformation sein. Diese Neugestaltung und Umgestaltung der alten Reformation kann jedoch nur ausder Hinwendung zum Ganzen, zur universalen, zur ökumenischen, zur wahrhaft katholischen Kirche kommen." *Reformation der Reformation in die Hochkirche* (1929), p. 365, quoted in: *Luther in Katholischer Sicht, Hessen* (Bonn, 1949), p. 38.

PREFACE

This book presents the commentaries on the widely-discussed "Twelve Evangelical * Affirmations of Catholic Truths" published in the seventh circular letter of the *Sammlung* ** in the summer of 1957, and eagerly awaited by Protestants and Catholics alike.

Twenty thousand copies of the Twelve Theses were circulated among Evangelical clergy and laity, arousing considerable interest when they were published. A long article appeared in the leading Catholic daily newspaper in Rome, *Il Quotidiano,* on July 11, 1957, regarding the aims of the *Sammlung* and the significance of the Twelve Theses, under the heading: "The End of the Protestant Reformation?" The German Catholic weekly, *Rheinischer Merkur* in the edition of August 2, 1957, stated: "Behind the Twelve Theses there is obviously a burning, spiritual passion for the unity of the Church, and behind this pas-

---

* The German word "Evangelische" which is most always rendered as "Evangelical" in this translation, when it is an adjective, can have a variety of meanings: sometimes "Lutheran"; at other times "Protestant"; and at still other times "Evangelical." Only when it appears as a noun has some liberty been taken in translating it as "Lutherans" or "Protestants" or "Evangelical Christians." The reader may wish to keep in mind that the word, out of the German context, presents certain difficulties in English.

** The word "sammlung," meaning literally "gathering" or perhaps "rally," is not really translatable into English and therefore the German form is kept throughout this translation. A brief summary of the origins and aims of the "sammlung" movement is presented immediately following this short preface.

sion are men and women, active, striving Christians, all of one mind and purpose, regardless of creed." The *Allgemeine Sonntagszeitung* of Würzburg, in the edition of July 7, 1957, declared: "The publishing of these Theses also made its impact upon us Catholics, penetrating to our very hearts."

The Twelve Theses, again presented in this book, deal with a number of important controversial issues: the Church's Christian mysteries, the mystery of the Church, the relation of grace and freedom, the sacrifice of Christ and the sacrifice of the Church, the apostolic succession of bishops, the office of the priesthood and ordination, the primacy of the Chair of Peter, the episcopal teaching office, the relation of Scripture and Tradition, the importance of the veneration of saints in the life of the Church.

The commentaries on the Theses, individually written by the various authors, appear in separate chapters with the following titles: The Call of Evangelical Christianity to Catholic Fulfillment; Catholic Truth in the New Testament, which is divided into two sections, The Life of the Church, and Order and Authority of the Church; Catholic Truth, Tradition and Ministry; The Significance of Lost Catholic Truths for the Life of the Church.

This book, the result of cooperative effort, gives us a complete theological explanation of what the *Sammlung* considers its purpose and task to be. The principal significance of this book, however, and its most stimulating aspect, is the call for a "Catholic Reformation" in the Evangelical Church, and likewise for a renewal of Catholicity in the Roman Church, in the spirit of the evangelical tradition.

The German Publisher
1958

The Sammlung

The *Sammlung* is an association of Evangelical men and women, clergy and laity, who have heard the divine call to reunite a divided Christendom and who accordingly pray and work in the hope that the reformed Churches, for their own fulfillment and also for the future welfare of the whole Church of God, may find their necessary place within the One, Holy, Catholic and Apostolic Church.

The members of the *Sammlung* are persuaded "that men must face the question of truth more earnestly than ever before, and they must acknowledge the fact that Reformation doctrine and likewise our whole ecclesiastical life are heavily weighted with misjudgments on both sides. . . . Therefore, a mutual acknowledgement must be made and a new relationship established with the pre-Reformation Roman Catholic Church, for we owe it to the welfare of the whole Church to make such an acknowledgement. Only in proportion as we thus take the question of truth seriously can we hope to overcome the differences between the Churches as well as those within Protestantism itself . . ."

The *Sammlung* arranges a conference of several days in the spring and fall of each year for friends and guests, providing daily religious services and prayers, and thorough consideration of controversial theological questions.

The earlier circular letters have now become a regular news-bulletin which keeps the friends of the *Sammlung* informed about the progress and problems of our work in both the Evangelical and the Roman Catholic Church.

Anyone wishing to know more about the *Sammlung*, or to become a member, may apply to one of the principal organizational centers at the following addresses: Provost

D. Hans Asmussen, Heidelberg, Häuserstrasse 39; Richard Baumann, Tübingen-Lustnau, Dorfstrasse 36; Rev. Ernst Fincke, Frankfurt/M, Töplitzstrasse 7; Gustav Huhn, Fürsteneck, Krs. Hünfeld/Hessen; Rev. Max Lackmann, Soest i. Westf., Thomästrasse 64; Rev. Wolfgang Lehmann, Offenbach a. M., Geleitstrasse 104.

We collect no membership dues from our friends but we ask for regular offerings to help pay the cost of our conferences and the publication of our news-bulletin; contributions should be made payable to the account of *Die Sammlung*, PSK 129 674, Frankfurt/M, Kurt Mink, Frankfurt/M, Bruchfeldstrasse 97.

CONTENTS

INTRODUCTION

by

HANS ASMUSSEN

What is the significance of this book? How did the *Sammlung* ever come into existence at all? Both questions belong together, and in the following pages several answers are given which attempt to set forth the fundamental principles and distinctive aims of our undertaking.

1) The *Kerygma,* the preaching of the Gospel in our Evangelical churches, is extremely vague and sometimes even heretical. This is true not only in regard to minor matters but also, and more particularly, concerning the question which the Reformation considered as the central issue of the Gospel: the question of salvation, which implies a determination to make our preaching widely effective, a purpose that is fully justified. But if, as a result of our public preaching, the question of how men may escape the wrath of God is no longer asked—and to a great extent this is the situation today—then the position of orthodoxy has been abandoned.

When, however, this question is still sometimes asked, answers are often given, even by competent persons, which can only be designated as heretical. Karl Barth, in his book, *Basel Sermons* (Baseler Predigten, May, 1957), published a Good Friday sermon which he preached in the Basel prison. He explained that *both thieves* together composed the first community of Jesus Christ. "For a Christian community can exist wherever there is a gathering of peo-

1

ple in the near presence of Jesus." It is true that only one of the thieves believed in Jesus, while the other reviled Him, but "this difference was not so important that it could affect the promise." Consequently, the apostle's saying can be applied to both thieves: *If we have died with Christ, we know that we shall also live with Him.* "It is certain," he continued, "that the two thieves, because they were both allowed to suffer and die with Him, were therefore both included in the promise."

We would not dare to preach in this way or in any similar manner. Certainly anyone who undertakes to live and die in accordance with this formula will be the loser. We cannot destroy the difference between belief and unbelief, established from all eternity. We dare not evade the question of God's wrath, and how to escape it, until we are at death's door. No one should therefore be offended if, because of our ordination vows, we deliberately seek those Churches, wherever they may be found, in which the old creed and the ancient meaning of the faith are still preached. There are—thank God!—still a number of Evangelical preachers of whom this may be said. But they are not the leaders. They do not set the tone. In the Roman Catholic Church, however, which confronts us everywhere in Germany, there is a vital concern regarding the coming judgment of God, and there is an awareness of the decisive difference between belief and unbelief. This is a very fundamental reason for our interest in this Church and everything occurring within it.

2) The remark is often heard among Lutherans in Germany that we have had to defend our very existence in two directions: in the east against Communism, and in the west against the Roman Catholic Church. We hear this kind of talk in the mouths of leading churchmen. But all

such talk is unfair, for it is an attempt to camouflage political neutrality with the halo of ecclesiastical martyrdom. It
is also detrimental to the Church because it leads people
to think and speak about the Catholic Church, not from
an ecclesiastical standpoint, but in the double-tongued
manner of political propaganda. In the same spirit, Evangelical youth groups of the Rhineland-Palatinate were in-
vited to hold discussions concerning the Roman Catholic
Church. Two examples of the guidance they were given
follow here: "It is not coincidental that Louis XIV, Na-
poleon, Hitler, Mussolini and Franco all were products of
a Catholic education. . . . No matter whether the Catholic
Church appears, for instance, as a great military power in
the Middle Ages or the Thirty Years' War, or as the richest
financial power in the world today, it was the first in history to introduce the methods of Big Business. . . . Ecumenical Protestants, of course, are strongly opposed to all
this. . . ."

There are Evangelical youth who are now receiving this
kind of instruction regarding the Church. With Søren
Kierkegaard, we can only say, "There was no one who
wept!" Is it any wonder that we should make the effort to
meet our fellow-Christians of the Catholic Church on another and more worthy level?

3) The Protestant Church of the Palatinate, a member
of the EKD (Evangelical Church in Germany), made an
agreement with the English Congregationalists permitting
the exchange of guest preachers and the mutual partaking
of the Lord's Supper. It is certainly doubtful whether this
is compatible with the fundamental law of the EKD,
which is supposed to be an association of Churches agree-
ing in matters of faith. Our Confession of Faith is Lutheran or Reformed, or both in the United Protestant

Church. But the Congregationalists profess neither the one nor the other. The Palatinate Churches which belong to the EKD have consequently made all of us wonder whether it is still valid to qualify Church membership according to the Confession of Faith as was customary heretofore. Moreover, inasmuch as the EKD has not objected to the decision of the Palatinate Churches, it may be assumed that a wholly new point of view in this matter has now been adopted. However, the authors of this book cannot accept this position. They believe that it indicates a strong trend toward the self-dissolution of Protestantism, and demands a neutralizing influence.

Therefore we are calling for a thorough understanding, or, even better, a real meeting with the Roman Catholic Church. It is a serious omen that the Palatinate decision was accepted so quietly by the German Evangelical Churches. What if some similar German ecclesiastical agreement is concluded with the Baptists or the Adventists? Would anyone even try to prevent it?

4) When the *Sammlung* began its work in January of 1954, it stood quite alone in its purpose and objective. It should not be forgotten that for years every serious approach to the Roman Catholic Church was viewed in Evangelical circles as a denial of faith, or was at least represented as such. In this respect, political factors played no small part. It was a time when Evangelical Church leaders found it very difficult to prove the Church's neutrality to the political parties. Many churchmen considered the Christian Democratic Union as the Catholic party, while the Trade Unions were accorded a place of primary importance in the strategy-planning of the leading Evangelical circles. Then followed the wave of interest in Eastern affairs. The rage for co-existence was limited, however,

to West Germany, for it never developed to any notable degree in the Soviet Zone. But Churches outside of Germany were also affected by it. How many traveled to Soviet Russia to visit the Patriarch, and what attractive reports they brought back! This whole movement—for one must call it that—completely collapsed during the period of domestic political crisis when the most prominent Evangelical leaders and groups had orientated themselves clearly to the political left.

For similar reasons we waited anxiously to see whether a single ecclesiastical voice would speak out for the Roman Catholic Church. The anti-Catholic propaganda against Spain and Colombia was in full swing. It was a masterful accomplishment to exploit for propaganda purposes those happenings in Spain and Colombia which were in any way comparable to the Soviet persecution of Christians. It was not until recently that there was any decline in this propaganda. However, this more enlightened outlook toward the world outside was narrowed by association with current internal German affairs. All of us still remember the whispering campaign against the Catholic Church: "Government posts are granted according to confessional, i.e. Catholic, allegiances." Even Evangelical Church leaders were openly making these accusations. There was the charge that the top positions in the Defense Ministry were held by Catholics, especially at a time when the country's defense was under the fiercest criticism of all parties that did not belong to the government coalition. Nevertheless, the *Sammlung* was never swept along with this tide, but in those years regarded the Catholic Church as a worthy partner for serious discussion and said so plainly.

5) Meanwhile, much has happened which allows us to consider everything in a different light. There is no need

to mention a large number of events; two will suffice. The Lutheran Bishops' Conference of Germany has appointed a Commissioner for Catholic Affairs, and the Lutheran World Alliance, meeting in Minneapolis, decided to participate in serious discussions with the Catholic Church and to establish an Institute for Interconfessional Questions. We can only appreciate the significance of both decisions if we realize that the Lutheran Church was responding to a similar overture on the part of the Catholic Church. The Catholic Bishops' Conference has for some years designated the Archbishop of Paderborn as their representative in these matters, and for some time there has been a Catholic Institute in Paderborn which is devoted to fostering relations between both Churches. It is of the greatest significance that the Lutheran Institute is sponsored not only by the Lutheran Church in Germany but by Lutheranism throughout the world. Inasmuch as the Lutheran Church has responded to the overtures of the Catholic Church in this manner, the positive approach to the Catholic Church has now received official approval and is no longer to be left to the free-lance "outsiders."

This is a far-reaching step forward, for no matter how we may designate the Evangelical position regarding the Catholic Church since the religious Peace of Augsburg in 1555, it was certainly never expected that Lutherans would give serious consideration to the Catholic Church at any time. Men were finished with the Catholic Church forever.

This attitude was carried to such extremes that the "No!" to Rome became modern Protestantism's only link with the Church of the sixteenth century. For many Protestants this is still true today. Many theologians and lay people no longer believe what the Lutheran Church believed and taught in the sixteenth century. But they are *against* Rome, and therefore certain that they have conclusively proved that they are Evangelical if not exactly Lutheran. The authors of this book cannot sanction this position. On the contrary, they rejoice over the two resolutions of the Lutheran conferences, and everything undertaken as a result of these resolutions will receive not only their greatest attention but their full support as well. Even if those in authority should encounter opposition to the resolutions regarding the Roman Catholic Church, as happened to ourselves, the important thing at this moment is the accomplishment which decisions of this kind represent. Here there can be no doubt. Because of these decisions the Lutheran Church is now moving toward the Roman Catholic Church in a way that has never occurred since its beginnings. The practical significance for the relationship of the Churches can be confidently left to Almighty God.

6) If Lutherans are seriously disposed to reach an understanding with the Catholic Church, it must first of all become apparent that the Lutheran Church in its beginnings was much more Catholic than it is today. We need only consider the teachings of our creed on Mary, the Mother of God. If they do not exactly occupy a central place, they are not however to be overlooked, and if the Lutheran Church really enters into relations with the Roman Catholic Church, then it must be asked whether we still accept these teachings of our own creed or not. Until now, nearly everyone in the Lutheran Church whose teachings about the Mother of God was the same as the Lutheran credal doctrine, was regarded as a Catholic in disguise. It is not long ago that a Lutheran bishop, although not in Germany, threatened a minister with ec-

clesiastical trial because he had referred to Mary as the Mother of God. The situation is similar regarding more basic doctrines. Some of these will be discussed in the following pages, but in general it must be admitted that the Lutheran Church will have to make new decisions concerning those things that are to be accepted as lawful and valid. The theology of the Reformation, so glibly mentioned in our day, is much too vague a concept to be used in holding any minister responsible for it, or to serve as a criterion of judgment. Moreover, it is not generally realized that the famous book, *De Servo Arbitrio,* still so freely quoted, is a complete contradiction of the most recent Lutheran theological works. If the Lutheran Church really intends to be true to itself, then it must complete the task that has remained unaccomplished from the start. The only way to Christian unity is through one's own creed and not by an evasion of it.

7) Under present circumstances a "Back-to-Luther" movement would help us very little. Our generation, or the coming generation, will have to make decisions which have never been made before. Some of these decisions will pertain to very essential matters. No appeal to the original Lutheran creed nor any return to Luther himself will be of any assistance. It cannot be denied that this is the true situation and has its basis in the fact that conditions have developed within the Lutheran Church which can never be compatible with the Lutheran creed. It is also an obvious fact that the Lutheran credal statements contain irreconcilable contradictions.

Article 28 of the Augsburg Confession teaches that the bishops, by divine right, have the power of jurisdiction, as it was generally understood in that era, in matters of faith and morals, but without any civil authority. But no

Lutheran Church exercised, or even wished to exercise this "divine right" during the past four hundred years. It is even doubtful whether there is today a single Lutheran bishop who understands his office according to this Article. Anyone halfway informed will know the historical origin and development of this situation, but there is absolutely no justification for it whatever. The authors of this book adhere to this Article of the Augsburg Confession even if they are consequently regarded as "Catholics."

This one example is sufficient to show that the Lutheran Churches are not Lutheran in the full sense of the Lutheran creed.

In regard to the contradictions in our creed we may refer to the Schmalkaldian articles which declare that the papacy was founded by the devil. Nevertheless, Melanchthon signed them with the observation that he was prepared to accept the pope as primate *by human right*. Äpin of Hamburg, in the name of all the pastors of that city, signed a statement based upon this reservation of Melanchthon.

It is impossible to reconcile contradictions like these. There simply is no way for us to accept a diabolical foundation of the Roman primacy, and therefore the Schmalkaldian treatise on the authority and primacy of the pope can no longer be regarded as the valid interpretation of the scriptural passages quoted by Melanchthon. Moreover, it must be remembered that Melanchthon's *apologia* is completely Catholic in tendency, as far as all these points are concerned. In fact, no credal writings of a later date have ever been as close to the Catholic faith as these. This is especially true of the doctrine of justification which he advocated, and when this is clearly understood there is nothing derogatory to be said about our beliefs. We need only keep in mind that these writings are the documents of a time of turmoil and revolution and they pertained to the particular conditions of those days in the hope that a suitable theological faculty would be established at some date to codify them all. However, this was a false hope. By 1555 there was practically no definite Lutheran doctrinal position, a condition that still remains unchanged. Instead, the fiction has been preserved that the Lutheran creed sets forth the Christian faith in its orthodox integrity, even though everyone knows that our Lutheran credal statements pertain only to particular questions. One of the aims of the authors of this book is to lay emphasis upon this fact.

8) We must go one step farther. Each of us learned in our youth to express the difference between the Catholic and Lutheran Churches in a very simple formula. It was customary, before the appearance of Karl Barth, to say that Catholics believe they are sanctified through good works, but Lutherans know they are saved by grace alone through faith. Anyone who has some respect for truth must readily admit that this formula is so false in its simplicity that it should never be allowed to be taught anywhere. The famous letter of Karl Barth to Hans Küng on the doctrine of justification marks the end of an inglorious period of Christian polemics.

In his first period Karl Barth tried to explain the difference between the two Churches by saying that the Catholic Church teaches the *analogia entis*—the analogy of being—which the Evangelical Church would necessarily reject. He meant that the Catholic Church saw an original relation between the created and the spiritual worlds which offers many possibilities for the perception of divine realities. For many years Barth's doctrine was considered as valid as dogma. There are many who believe it even now. Meanwhile, however, in careful terms Karl Barth has made an essential modification of the doctrine. His latest treatment of this subject can be found in his book on the humanity of God, *Die Menschlichkeit Gottes* (Zollikon, 1956).

We are wholly skeptical of every attempt to reduce the differences between the two Churches to any simple formula. For it is a life process which divides the Churches, and although a certain theoretical knowledge is also required, we know that life processes can never be fully reduced to any verbal formula. This may be a disturbing fact, but it cannot be ignored. Anyone who really believes that the differences between the Churches can be expressed in a simple statement should be asked to explain where the saving presence of Christ may be found today. Must we deny this presence in the Catholic Mass? Or would Catholics say that it cannot be found in the Lutheran's Lord's Supper? It seems to us that this is the important question. Everyone who gives serious thought to the matter will see that it is extremely complex because it is dependent on many different points of view.

9) Some theologians say that the authors of this book are neither qualified nor competent to conduct Catholic-Evangelical discussions because we are not typically Evangelical. But a judgment of this kind should only be made with considerable caution, for the essential character of the Evangelical Church will be lost if the individual no longer has the right to exercise private judgment in regard to doctrine and to form opinion based on Holy Scripture. If this criticism were directed against us by Catholics, we would have to agree to some extent, but when the accusation comes from Lutherans themselves, it neces-

sarily becomes a falsification of the very essence of Evangelicalism. The primary vocation of Evangelicalism cannot be realized if we refuse to exercise private judgment. If we are to follow the course originally chosen, we must adhere to this principle to the very end. We should be glad whenever private judgment is exercised by anyone at all.

In this book there will be a great deal of theological discussion in the strict sense of the term, and the conventional language of scientific theology will often be used. But the parochial pastor will also have something to say and will express himself in a manner that is customary for pastors of parish churches. It would be a serious diminution of the Church's breadth of truth to do otherwise, for it pertains to the very essence of the Church to allow all the many kinds of vocational activity and experience to have a full place in her life and this necessarily implies the right to be heard. This is not the place to express an opinion concerning the relative worth of these various vocational activities, but it must be said that Christian reality is necessarily diminished if the kind and manner of discussion that is called scientific becomes absolute. This is particularly true of the subject matter of this book. If a divided Christendom can find the way to reunion, it should be the concern of all Christians everywhere and not merely of some particular or professional group. The authors of this book are not all of one type, but the central theme of the book is a bond of unity between them. We share a common conviction that the Catholic Question is *the* question of our generation. With the same seriousness whereby we are committed to the entire Credo as a declaration of faith, we believe that the unity of Christ's Church is the manifest will of God.

It is our opinion that the concerns of a pastor in the exercise of his ministry should receive as much attention in this matter as theological considerations in the restricted sense.

If we are regarded as essentially Catholics already, it is difficult to say whether this is reproach or praise. We really hope that our critics will also realize the importance of being Catholics themselves, for otherwise they would not be within the communion of the universal Church. The author of this Introduction cannot keep silent about his own experience in this respect. He discovered indisputable evidence that there has been a fundamental change in Evangelical Churches in their attitude toward the Catholic Movement among us, and notably since 1948. When, at the beginning of the Second World War, he gave public talks in Lichterfelde on the Roman Catholic Mass and its critical evaluation in Lutheran credal statements, and somewhat later published his book on the Church and the Ministry, *Die Kirche und das Amt* (Kaiser-Verlag), he hardly said anything different than would be said today, but this did not become a hindrance or a detriment in representing the Evangelical Church in its relations with the National Socialist State, and after 1945 he held one of the highest posts in the Evangelical Church of Germany. Meanwhile, if the situation has changed, then we must be permitted to inquire how this change in German Evangelical attitudes can be explained.

10) The simplest and most damaging criticism of our undertaking seems to be the opinion that the *Sammlung* leads all its followers straight down the Road to Rome, and "as everyone knows," Rome considers unconditional submission as the only conceivable solution of the ecclesiastical question. This criticism, however, is not as simple

as it sounds. There is no easy way out whatever. Those who criticize us in this way should ask themselves whether they have not allowed a basic law, essential to Evangelicalism to be completely forgotten. This law is constitutive for all Evangelical life; it is the law of freedom of speech in the Church. It is an historical fact that in our generation and for a long time before, only a small number of Evangelical theologians could ever present their message in a way that would make it available to Catholics. Neither the classical Lutheran dogmatics, nor the old or new Erlanger School were successful in this; the Bensheimer Institute need hardly be mentioned. But why do we deny our Roman Catholic brethren the same consideration that is granted so generously to any primitive tribe and even to the declared enemies of the very idea of God?

In this book there are certain questions which, among others, were proposed to the Roman Catholic Church, and it can be shown that all of them were given a fair hearing by that Church. This only proves that men will listen attentively to any voice that sounds the note of love. Should not the critics therefore re-examine their own manner of speaking in reference to the Catholic Church? It is strange that anyone would really want to bring any accusation against us merely because we at least make the effort to approach the Roman Catholic Church with love. Accusations of this kind should never be made in the era of the Church.

We would like to be rid of the impression that most Evangelical theologians are reluctant to enter into serious discussions with Roman Catholics because they are afraid of embarrassment, more especially concerning their own beliefs. In the Roman Catholic Church there are zealous prayers said for all Protestants, and if we would also pray fervently for Roman Catholics, we would soon be able to speak with them.

Everything pertaining to the dread "unconditional surrender" to Rome is, so to speak, a matter which to the greatest extent concerns the Lutheran Church *itself*. Vague catchwords of salvation, shameful silence about the legitimate hope for unity, the failure of the bishops to act effectively, especially on neglect or abuse of the sacraments, even though empowered by Article 28 of the Augsburg Confession with the full right and duty to do so, all force the Roman Catholic Church more and more into a rigid position. In this position *Catholicism,* as a system, wins out over a genuine Catholic attitude. The more Catholic we become, ourselves, the less we have to fear the challenge of "unconditional surrender." Søren Kierkegaard says that the Lutheran Reformation was meant to be a corrective movement within the Roman Catholic Church, but if this corrective becomes a fixed condition, then it will bring about the very undoing of the Church. This is unquestionably true, for we can never be rid of the Catholic Church. We have come forth from this Church, and within her communion alone can we find our fulfillment. In the measure in which this occurs we will also accomplish our corrective mission. In the same degree will a Catholic Reformation be finally achieved.

With this hope in mind we publish our seven circular letters once again, and with this same hope and purpose the five contributions of the several authors of the seventh letter and its theses present a particular point of view. It was not possible for us to touch upon each and every statement of the theses, but this does not mean that any of our "Evangelical Affirmations of Catholic Truths" are unimportant for salvation. We know that many inquiries will necessarily come our way, and we look forward to them and will gladly reply to all of them. We are fully aware of our shortcomings, but we are nevertheless convinced that the Evangelical-Catholic relationship has never before been presented or discussed in this particular manner, and, therefore, what we have to say will afford an opportunity that should not be neglected.

THE SEVEN CIRCULAR LETTERS

IN THE ERA OF THE CHURCH

I

Duty and conscience compel us to write to all who share our concern, inviting them to consider with us a number of questions concerning the Christian Church and especially Evangelical Christianity. Certain truths are in the hearts of all men, but the voice which ought to form these thoughts into words is still silent. We are convinced that this paralyzing silence must now be brought to an end. That is why we are sending these letters out to you.

1

It is right and fitting that our Churches are profoundly concerned about matters pertaining to this present world. But we will not deny the feeling that the way in which this concern is actually expressed has aroused our most serious doubts. Not only are many political decisions a hard blow to the Church, but it also seems evident that the Church's own performance would indicate a lack of authority to correct abuses or even to give guidance to troubled consciences. This defect is deeply rooted. The Apostle says that the Church is the pillar and ground of truth. Can we say this about our own Church too? There must be an unhealthy condition at the very heart of things when the Church becomes a mere figure of vacillation.

17

Surely it is time that we speak quite openly and seriously about this fact. It has become necessary that all of us, into whose hearts God has given love for the Church, should now think earnestly about this situation and work diligently to make everything different and better.

We believe that in our era the Church's vacillating aspect is due entirely to a lack of unity. In this divided condition most people resign themselves to allowing the unity of the Body of Christ to remain obscure. This Body was sacrificed for us and ought to be present among us as one corporate body, with the unity of one Lord, one Faith and one Baptism manifest to all.

2

We implore you to consider carefully with us whether it is not an easy rationalization to look resignedly upon the disunion of the Body of Christ as something regrettably unavoidable. How can we make a prayer out of resignation? How can we come to grips with the problem if we are resigned to it? Is that not simply lack of obedience and faith?

Our lack of faith indicates several things:

a) We are completely satisfied if our Church, which calls itself a reformed communion, is not even in agreement with the Church of the Lutheran Reformation. Is there any way to justify so much resistance to the praiseworthy efforts among us to restore the full divine service of the Lutheran Mass and the central importance of the holy sacraments and confession? Many Lutheran communities and churches are deprived of guidance in matters of faith according to their creed. Certainly all Lutherans of good will should desire above all else to return now, and with repentance, to our own starting-point.

b) We act as if the Church had never existed until 1517. Are we really quite ready to abandon the great values of the pre-Reformation Church? All of us have good reason to remind ourselves of the apostolic origin of the bishop's office, and to learn new respect for the great gifts which God has given to all Christendom and all people through monasticism. How many of us still remember that it was St. Boniface who converted the Germans to Christianity and that our own link with the Apostles cannot omit this Saint or any of the other Catholic missionaries?

c) We dispense ourselves from great parts of the truth that was the possession of the apostles and the prophets. But do we really have the right to conceal the truth that grace builds on nature and therefore comes to us as grace through created reality? It may be asked who actually authorizes our continual suppression of the teaching of the reward of good deeds. How can we fully convince ourselves that the preaching of the Gospel, the priestly function at divine worship, and the martyrdom of Christians, are no longer in our eyes a continuation and sharing of Christ's sacrifice? Strictly speaking, how do we dare to allow Peter's See to become the sole concern of students of ancient languages and of historians in the schools? It is precisely our disbelief that makes us see the Church in a purely secular way. That is why we do not perceive the spiritual mystery within her, or live in the communion of the saints and of the spirits of just men made perfect.

Will you not agree that the awareness of our deficiencies should now finally lead us to certain definite conclusions about them? In this letter we have written nothing that has not been common knowledge for a long time among those participating in Evangelical theological research. But our Church seems to look upon this research as a kind of private enterprise for specialists whose interests are strictly theological.

3

It is however a real adversity for ecclesiastical life in these times that so many among us deliberately reject the new knowledge derived from the studies that we and many other Christians have made in regard to the Roman Catholic Church. Relations with this Church ought to be the special concern of German Christians because we have the particular duty of living and working in close proximity with Roman Catholics everywhere in our own country.

It does seem almost incredible that the two largest denominations act as if nothing had ever happened to make them even aware of each other, and yet all German-speaking people gratefully receive the gospel message in literature, on the radio, and in publications from both Evangelical and Roman Catholic sources. On the Last Day the Lord will not forget that Christians of both Churches have equally suffered as brethren and yet this has been quite forgotten in less than ten years. We certainly do not claim that the two great Christian communions in Germany are ready for reunion now. We know that the truth still stands between us. But we also know that truth stands between Evangelical communities and Evangelical theologians as well. In this respect our relations with the Roman Catholic Church are not unique. Perhaps, however, we still reproach the Church of Rome because, unlike most Evangelical Churches, she proclaims boldly articles of faith as binding upon all Christians and as truths that are essential to our life in this present world. On the other hand, we implore our Roman Catholic brethren to tell us in what way their possession of a faith puts us in a weaker position for reaching the full light of Christ, which they enjoy. For this is all that really matters.

4

If you believe, as we do, that all these questions have revealed a whole series of problems demanding solution in our time, and especially in Germany, then please let your address be known to one of the undersigned. We know very well that similar questions have been under consideration throughout this country and beyond it. But there has not yet been any united action by like-minded people, and tomorrow may well be too late.

Perhaps you have already found some group or other who are deeply concerned about these very problems. In that event, please put us in touch with them. As soon as we have some general idea of the people and places that are interested in these same questions, we shall begin preparations for a meeting that will bring us together. Perhaps it will be necessary to organize a smaller group whose members will be assigned particular duties and tasks, but first of all we must let the call of this letter be proclaimed as loudly as possible wherever German is spoken. We shall be writing again soon to discuss in detail the various problems set forth in this letter.

Offenbach/Main
Second Sunday after Epiphany, 1954

Dr. Hans Asmussen, D.D.
Pastor Max Lackmann
Pastor Ernst Fincke
Pastor Wolfgang Lehmann

II

We are often asked what we are really seeking, and our answer must express our intention as clearly as possible in this time of general perplexity.

1

We want the call, *Christ Alone!* to be clearly heard through the whole Church, and we want this call to be accepted and effectual. But we do not mean Christ in separation from the Father and the Holy Spirit. We possess Christ alone solely *in* the Father and *through* the Holy Spirit. Christ acts in no other way. He redeems and renews us through His created body and the Church.[1] No one may have God for his Father who does not also have the Church for his Mother. *Christ Alone!* can only mean *Christ and the Church.*[2]

Christ's sacrifice alone is an affirmation that tells us that every follower of Christ becomes both priest and victim through His sacrifice.[3] "He who hears you, hears me"

[1] The Evangelical declaration, *Christ Alone!* is not a direct contradiction of the Catholic phrase, *Christ and the Church*. Various theologians, as for example Karl Barth and Helmut Thielecke, are now concerned about this question which was insufficiently recognized by the Reformation. But in no way have they placed such emphasis upon the word "and" as Holy Scripture requires.

[2] The word "and" should be understood in the sense of E. Käsemann's statement in his work on the Body of Christ, *Leib und Leib Christi* (1933), page 156: "According to the epistles to the Ephesians and Colossians we possess Christ in no other way except in His Body, the Church. To this extent the Church is identical with Christ." But this should also be compared with the comment of G. Jacob in *Evangelische Theologie* (1952-53), page 202: "Nevertheless, the identity of Christ with His Church may not be proclaimed."

[3] Compare this with Martin Luther's *Sermon vom neuen Testament* (*Clemen I*, 314 F., WA 6, 369F). "Not that we offer the sacrament, but

(Lk. 10:16), is the real meaning of *Christ's Word Alone!*
His liturgy, bidding us to make God's whole creation serve
Him for His glorification in liturgy and life, is the full
implication of *Christ's Worship Alone!* [4] Finally, the stir-
ring cry, *Christ Alone!*, reminds us that there is only *one*
Body of Christ in heaven and on earth, in order that all
men may know that the Father has sent the Son (Jn. 17:23).

2

We want the call, *Through Grace Alone!* to be clearly
heard through the whole Church, and we want this call
to be accepted and effectual. But we do not want men to
think that supernatural grace can be separated from its
effect upon and through created beings.[5] We only live
through grace alone when, as creatures made in the image
of God, we are free for the service of God. Through grace
alone are we created for good works and are made holy,

---

through our praise, prayer and sacrifice we give Him a reason and in-
ducement to offer Himself for us in heaven and ourselves together with
Him . . . consequently, I also offer Christ that I may desire and believe
that He accepts me with my prayer and praise, and through Himself
presents them before God. He gives me a sign to confirm my faith that
He is willing to do this. The sign is the sacrament of bread and
wine. It is therefore evident that the priest alone does not offer Mass,
but each and everyone does so through his own faith, for this is the
true, priestly office through which Christ is offered to God."

[4] In this sentence the liturgy of Creation (Psalm 148) and of Jesus'
Death (Hebrews 8:6) and the Church (Phil. 2:17) are seen as a unity, as
in the Apocalypse (5:6-10). The binding nexus is the sacrament "in which
the Church consummates the unity of her earthly and heavenly form"
(Karl Barth, in *Kirkliche Dogmatik II*, 1, 180). See also E. Stauffer's book,
Theologie des Neuen Testaments (3rd edition, page 293).

[5] This statement is directed against the opinion which has now become
almost a dogma, that grace can be granted only as a personal gift of God.
On the contrary, Peter speaks of "all grace" (I Pet. 5:10) or "manifold
grace" that is to be administered (4:10).

and consequently we can sanctify all things through the Word of God and prayer.[6] However, we cannot countenance any of the talk about grace which does not take creation and its order into account, as if the grace of God could save us wholly apart from everything that God created and sustains. We know that God wills that grace shall come to us through created things. In this world the idea of grace apart from creation is wholly imaginary.

Through grace alone has the larger meaning of *God and His saints,* for all good things performed by the saints are the work of God. It is God's will that every good deed to be done in the world will be accomplished only by His saints, and this is a further meaning of the phrase, *through grace alone.*[7] It has the work of the Church and her divine offices in its full implication.[8] To be saved by grace, and judged according to our works is not a contradiction.[9]

[6] Consult D. Bonhoeffer's *Ethik* (1949), page 254: "The isolation of the person from the world of things is idealistic, not Christian. Christ does not redeem the person from the world of things, but from the world of sin; these are two very different realities."

[7] The New Testament refers to the angels and to faithful believers as *saints,* and more especially the apostles and charismatics (Käsemann, *op. cit.,* page 146). The Apocalypse of John shows how all of these *saints* participate in everything that God does.

[8] Ephesians 4:7-12. Grace becomes objective in the organized and hierarchical reality of the Church whose ministry and jurisdiction became effective immediately after the Ascension. In this connection there is new light on the primacy of Peter which the Lord proclaimed in Matthew 16:18 and in Luke 22:31.

[9] Compare with H. Hofer's commentary on the Pauline doctrine of justification in the light of new research, in his book, *Die Rechtfertigungsverkündigung des Paulus nach neuerer Forschung* (1940). He shows how this differs from the confessional writings of the sixteenth century. We must also note the attempt at a dialectical interpretation of the New Testament preaching on grace and judgment in W. Joest's study of law and freedom, *Gesetz und Freiheit* (1951), page 169 ff.

3

We want the call, *The Bible Alone!* to be clearly heard through the whole Church, and we want this call to be accepted and effectual.

But we do not want Holy Scripture to be dissociated from the authorship of God or from its inseparable connection with the Church. Scripture has God for its author through the inspiration of the Holy Spirit and is entrusted to the stewardship of the Church. The commendable work of science on Holy Scripture would inevitably deteriorate if it were no longer in agreement with the interpreting Church. Theologians would then be eliminating from Scripture whatever was contrary to their system and theory. Quoting John against Matthew, and Paul against Luke and James, deprives the Church of Scripture in its fulness and its diversity.[10] Consequently, we want the Church to sincerely recognize the obligation of sound scriptural exegesis, for it is the Church's duty to explain everything in the Bible which is binding upon us.[11] Evangelical theo-

[10] H. Diem, in *Grundfragen der biblischen Hermeneutik* (1950), page 34, a study of the basic questions of Biblical Hermeneutics, declares, ". . . the conception according to Luke is the tendency that leads to Catholicism and must eliminate the Paul of the Epistles. If one decides for Paul, the beginning of a mistaken development must be seen in the viewpoint of Luke." O. Bauernfeind, in *Evangelische Theologie* (1953) page 349, tells us, "Where Paul does not concern himself entirely with Christ he is theologically less relevant." P. Althaus, in his *Christlichen Wahrheit I*, 211 ff., thinks that the New Testament must be critically examined in regard to "Catholic" ideas. In the section on woman's work in the Lutheran World Federation, dealing with matrimonial questions, Hahn's *Partnerschaft* (1953), page 54, affirms that Paul, in some places, "does not reach the full height of the Gospel."

[11] See P. Brunner, *Schrift und Tradition* (1951), in which the question of tradition is taken very seriously. The crisis in Evangelical exegetical tradition was emphasized even more strongly by G. Glöege in his lecture, "Revelation and Tradition" on the occasion of the Berlin Theologian's Day. Contrary to the absolute prinicple of "the Bible and the Bible

logians of our day are either right or wrong when they
claim to find "Catholic" doctrine in many parts of Holy
Scripture. If they are right, then our Church must allow
itself to be changed and corrected. If, however, the theologians are wrong, it is then the responsibility of our
Church to give us clear instruction on these points. For
we are obliged to preach the whole content of the Bible.
Our Evangelical traditions and teachings must be subject
to the judgment of Scripture in its entirety. We cannot
evade the issue by substituting the "Tidings of the Reformation" or a "New Testament Kerygma" in place of
Scripture itself.

4

We are convinced that no one can be faithful to the Lutheran creed unless he accepts these conclusions. The rup-
ture of what should be an indissoluble relationship
between Christ and His Church, between creation and
supernatural grace, between Holy Scripture and the history of the Church, has resulted in diminishing the authority of the Lord as well as the power of grace and Scripture
in the Evangelical Church. In this respect, the following
word of Scripture is especially pertinent: "And he did not

Only!" and the subjectivism and unhistorical biblicism of the older
Protestantism, Gloege pointed out the relation between revelation and
tradition, explaining that tradition is a function of the community which
is formed by revelation. "We must understand revelation as an active
event which is perpetuated orally . . . therefore, tradition is the form in
which the Church lives through the period between the Ascension and
the Second Coming. The Son is manifested through revelation which God
links with the historical tradition. There can be no subjectivity of understanding without conceptual assumptions. Revelation lives on as a
tradition that has been preached, heard, understood and attested. Therefore the traditional understanding of Scripture always appertains wholly
to the revelation in Scripture." G. Harder, in *Die Zeichen der Zeit* (1954),
page 143.

many mighty works there because of their unbelief" (Mt. 13:58). Our profession of faith binds us to the apostolic Christianity of pre-Reformation times. If this were not so, we would be merely a separated sect.

We claim that we have expressed the authentic voice of the holy, apostolic and Catholic Church. Our divergence from others has now become obvious. The Synodal Address on the Barmen Declaration of 1934, interpreting the latter theologically as binding, in accord with the will of the Synod, is a guarantee that our own testimony is legitimately derived from this Declaration.

Kiel, Easter, 1954

> Dr. Hans Asmussen, D.D.
> Pastor Max Lackmann
> Pastor Ernst Fincke
> Pastor Wolfgang Lehmann

III

Months have passed since we sent our last circular letter. We wanted to give thorough consideration to everything and to avoid the anticipation of developments. We have now become more sure of ourselves, and many things are clearer to us all. Many people have found their way to us.

We must now go forward, step by step, because much has happened that will no longer allow us to stand still.

A delegation of Evangelical church leaders has visited Soviet Russia and established closer contact with the Russian Orthodox Church there. But that is not all! Our Evangelical leaders and the Russian Orthodox hierarchy have agreed to authorize joint study-weeks, the interchange of books and publications, and the exchange of theology students also. We must remember, however, that the Russian Orthodox Church is much closer to the Roman Catholic Church in many points of belief and practice than to any Evangelical Church, and more especially in their conception of the Sacrifice of the Mass and their devotion to Mary, the Mother of God.

Dr. Dibelius, the Protestant bishop of Berlin, chairman of the Council of the EKD (Evangelical Church in Germany) and member of the principal assembly of the Ecumenical Movement, paid a visit to the Pope in Rome while on his way to Australia to attend a meeting of the World Council of Churches.

Both men expressed the common intention of fighting against Godlessness. In the whole history of the Church there is no similar example of a high-ranking official of a non-Catholic Church calling upon the Pope in a visit of this kind.

Provost Grüber, who only a few weeks ago tried to induce the Evangelical Church to recognize the government of the German Democratic Republic of the Soviet Zone *(Stuttgarter Zeitung)* is now willing to relinquish his post as commissioner of the EKD to the Soviet government of East Germany.

Our Church president, Dr. Niemöller, has announced his resignation from the board of the EKD. The administration of the Church's foreign relations is said to be in different hands now *(Evangelischer Presse Dienst, Frankfurt)*. The press claims to have knowledge that Dr. Niemöller is being considered for the post of commissioner of the EKD to the Soviet regime of the German Democratic Republic. It is characteristic, of course, for the daily press to publicize news of this kind, and if the news is correct, it is hoped that Dr. Niemöller will perform his task in close cooperation with Bishop Dibelius. Meanwhile, the persecution of Christians in the German Democratic Republic continues.

There has been an unexpected change in the relationship of the Christian Churches with one another, although many are not aware of this. In the face of mounting threats, with which they become increasingly more experienced, the Churches are beginning to think seriously about the need to draw closer together than was ever thought possible heretofore. This kind of thinking has found expression in writing also. In a book that received considerable notice and comment, a Protestant theologian wrote about the Roman Catholic Church in glowing terms: "Truly, the Catholic Church has at all times been the abode of the Gospel and is so today" (Löwenich, *Der moderne Katholizismus*). Such a statement plainly indicates the complete change occuring in our time. We may not be able to agree with the same author in his opinion, which he considers very important, that the Protestant Church has "the dual task of preaching the Gospel while also maintaining a close identification with modern science in its universal sensitivity to truth." However, we can be grateful to him and to others for making the Catholic Church a real issue in our thinking today. We are thankful that we Lutherans have become a real issue also! The time when one Church regarded the other as a necessary evil should be over forever, for the Churches have now undertaken to help one another toward the attainment of an authentic Christian outlook and attitude, in order that they may go forward into the future as one Body of Christ in the unity of a common faith. It is true, however, that we must now realize with sadness that relations between the Churches have deteriorated in more recent years. Indeed, there have been deliberate efforts to bring this about. On the other hand, there have been contacts which we cannot ignore between Lutherans and Catholics which have made us experience the reality of Christ. These experiences will never allow any of us to turn back. They have facilitated and made possible the necessary theological effort which we are carefully pursuing and must continue in order that we may lay hold of the real significance of the experiences given to us. This must be done not only for our own understanding, but also for the sake of other people who will ultimately be able to share them through our common witness.

We must always be mindful of the folly and enmity of the devil and the world. They would stop at nothing to thwart this movement toward unity. We dare not allow ourselves to be led astray, and if the temptations which assail us are not more than we can bear, we should be grateful that we are able to overcome and resist them.

More than ever before, we need prayers and help, criticism and encouragement. We are all sharply aware of the fact that we have entered into unexplored territory. But we also know that many of the clergy and laity are of one mind with us, considering the movement of the Churches toward reunion as the only right course, to be taken immediately and with deep conviction. Both the letters and the material help that we have received indicate this clearly. We are sending this letter to let you know that we are still hard at work, and as joyfully as ever. But we would like to ask all of you to labor zealously in rallying all those who are longing for the manifestation of Christ and the unity of His Body.

We need to remember always that we are under biblical

command to keep ever in mind the people who are suffering because of the divided condition of the Churches, and particularly our own brethren in the Soviet Zone where it is most obvious that all the Churches must take their stand together. In West Germany the divisions among Christians also afford new cause daily to obstruct and impede the sound reconstruction of our commonwealth, and this must be strongly resisted. *Let us all join in the great task together!*

Offenbach/Main, February 17, 1956

> Dr. Hans Asmussen, D.D.
> Pastor Max Lackmann
> Pastor Ernst Fincke
> Pastor Wolfgang Lehmann

IV

The last synod of the United Evangelical Lutheran Church, meeting in Hanover, took up the problem of the Roman Catholic Church. If we may regard this fact alone as a definite step forward, it will seem even more significant when we note that the problem was considered in special relation to tolerance. Bishop Dietzfelbinger of Bavaria delivered an important address to the synod which was given due regard by our Catholic brethren. We are told that discussions between Catholics and Protestants will now be sponsored by the Lutheran Church like those established earlier by the German Evangelical Church. The Lutheran Bishops' Conference in September is to make a final decision about this. It could almost be considered sensational that a delegation of Roman Catholic visitors was present in Hanover, participating in fruitful talks that were held apart from the regular sessions.

The *Sammlung* has learned of these new endeavors with gratitude, for we can only welcome such an increase of real communication with our separated brethren. It seems worth considering whether the new discussion groups should not concentrate upon the situation in Bavaria, because in no other Federal State do the Churches meet at such close range, sometimes in matters of common difficulty or common need.

We hope that the Bishops' Conference will find the best solution to the problem now, and we shall do all we can to encourage, rather than hinder, the work that has been undertaken.

In Hanover the *Una Sancta* movement was considered to be an unsuitable approach, as the *Una Sancta* is largely Roman Catholic in orientation. But is this opinion really justifiable? More prayers for the unity of Christendom are certainly offered by Roman Catholics. But while we are for the most part quite convinced of the unassailability and unchangeableness of the Catholic position, it is nevertheless a position that seems very strange and even alarming to Protestants generally. This is the reason for the uneasy, sensitive, and skeptical feelings among Lutherans. However, we should ask ourselves what is being accomplished *by Lutherans* to develop a healthy and helpful relationship between Catholics and Protestants. If we find that we are doing nothing at all, or very little, can we seriously complain because others are accomplishing more than we? This should be given some careful thought. Until recently there was no Lutheran inter-Church activity or relationship with Roman Catholics. We need to reach a better understanding of the *Una Sancta* movement. Are the members and friends of the *Sammlung* active in the movement now? Our Roman Catholic brethren take it for granted that we are. But is it really true? If *Una Sancta* be the unorganized movement which for a long while heretofore has been rallying all those who think it shameful that Christians do not belong to *one* Church, then it may be correctly said that we too belong to *Una Sancta*. But if *Una Sancta* is considered as a specific organization with a sphere of work that does not allow for an authentic Evangelical inquiry into Roman Catholic Christianity, then we do not belong. This is not to underestimate the great debt of gratitude owed by all Christians to men like the late Dr. Metzger and His Excellency, Abbot Emmanuel Heufelder, O.S.B., of Niederaltaich, for reviving a work that had long been dormant. After all, for people who are interested in the aims and efforts of *Una Sancta,* the group or movement which happened to be called by this name was the only one that was concerned about the same problems and questions. Lutheran critics of our day should keep this clearly in mind.

The *Sammlung* did not formally join the *Una Sancta* movement, but this did not diminish our readiness for willing cooperation. From the very beginning we kept separate name lists, according to Church affiliations, and regarded the Lutheran membership as the principal strength of our endeavor. It should be apparent that this was a beginning that would ultimately develop into something of importance in the future. Our idea is essentially to foster a kind of inter-Church endeavor in which the members of each Church who are willing to participate actively will work first of all among other members of their own Church. In view of the divided condition of Christendom, which Church would not be primarily concerned about its own position and its own mistakes? We should try to imagine the great change that would follow in the relations between the Churches if the Christians of one denomination would no longer see the others in the distorted image of four hundred years ago, but as they really are today! This would surely bring about a tremendous transformation in our whole conception of the Church.

With these thoughts in mind, we must make the emphatic demand that troubled consciences be taken seriously in all of our Evangelical Churches. Certainly this should be the special obligation of a Church which derives its very name from Dr. Martin Luther. For many years Evangelical Christians, including leading churchmen, theologians, pastors and laymen from all walks of life, have come forward seeking help and guidance. In private discussions and at Church gatherings, in publications and in formal addresses, serious questions arising from various difficulties of conscience have been asked regarding traditional Evangelical beliefs. The number of those who are unable to perceive the realization of Christ's message in the traditional forms of ecclesiastical organization, divine service, and confessional truths is increasing year by year. These people are no longer able to find a real home in their parochial communities and Churches. Disciplinary measures, defamations, vain promises and the general silence regarding notable conversions are no proof of courage or of strength. Those who are troubled or conscience-stricken must be either bound or freed, and those who insist upon maintaining the *status quo* at all costs, and will not admit that we have a great deal to learn, perhaps even from the Roman Catholic Church, will be primarily responsible if the Evangelical Churches finally cease to exist.

At the Church Rally in Frankfurt it was the laity above all who were especially interested in auricular confession. This should convince us that there need be no further reluctance to discuss controversial issues that arise among our own people.

If we really hope to make progress in this difficult undertaking, we will open our gates wide so that the stimulus for reunion of the separated Churches can truly come from the lay people themselves. This seems particularly important to us, for the Church consists not only of theologians but also of a great company of layfolk whose tongues must be loosened. Once again the Frankfurt Rally proved that the laity under certain circumstances will speak more clearly, more courageously, and more truthfully than their pastors. Surely it is now time that we ask laymen who are interested in ecclesiastical matters their opinions concerning the relationship of the two largest Churches. The many letters we have received on this subject have convinced us that the laity, more than ever before, feel compelled to express themselves freely in regard to these matters. A frank and genuine discussion must take place between the leaders of the Churches and the lay people concerning inter-Church relations. We feel that these questions should be openly discussed in larger gatherings and assemblies also. At the larger gatherings, however, it often happens that the laity hardly get a chance to speak because, as a matter of fact, only a few theologians carry on the discussions, and the talks are generally meant primarily for a theological elite rather than for laymen. We have much to learn in this regard.

If *special representatives for inter-Church work* were appointed in the various regional districts of the Church, like the ministers who have already been chosen for social problems, youth work, marriage counseling, etc., the work could then proceed much more smoothly than at present. It would no longer be so readily suspected of engaging in mere proselytism or spreading Evangelical defeatism. Moreover, our Churches would be giving open proof of their real approval of interdenominational responsibility. At this time it may all sound like building castles in the air, but it is worth considering nevertheless. It must surely seem ridiculous that discussions of religious belief and practice with Jews, Mohammedans, Chinese, and Papuans are accepted as something quite normal, while at the same time those who wish to talk seriously with their Catholic brethren about the unity of the Church are objects of suspicion. Have we completely forgotten that according to Our Lord's own word the success of missionary endeavor depends on overcoming the divisions among us? The goal of our pioneer Evangelical missionaries of the nineteenth century was not regarded as less utopian than the goal of a reunited Christendom today. Nevertheless, our Church now values missionary effort as the obvious work of faith of the true Church of Christ.

Common meetings with our separated brethren would also be much more fruitful if we had done a certain amount of preparatory work among members of our own Church. For example, it would not be proper to wish for discussions with Roman Catholics concerning problems that pertain to devotion to Mary, as long as we are not really certain about our own Evangelical beliefs regarding the Mother of God. This is a subject that still requires considerable theological study in its various aspects.

If the Catholic element has occasionally been predominant in the *Una Sancta* discussions in the past, it is only because the Catholic authorities have for a long time allowed certain arrangements which legitimize inter-Church activity as a matter of principle. We could mention, for instance, the Chair of Unity Octave of prayer for the reunion of Christendom which is but little observed in Evangelical circles. If our Church authorities would promote this kind of ecclesiastical endeavor they would do much to restore inter-Church activities and would influence the larger, mutual efforts in a free and healthy way. Furthermore, they would formulate our doctrinal positions in such a way that we could, in accordance with Our Lord's word, enter into discussions with any of our brethren who are opposed to us for any reason at all. We have never succeeded in doing this yet.

Meanwhile the work of the *Sammlung* continues its course. We have not restricted ourselves to any particular area of activity; however, we are not overlooking any field of work that has been neglected by others. It seemed only right that we should bring all of these many considerations to the attention of our friends. It is entirely possible that some of our objectives can soon be attained.

We are now looking forward to the coming conference discussions in Fürsteneck. Remember the conference in your prayers even if you cannot attend.

Offenbach/Main, August 18, 1956

> Dr. Hans Asmussen, D.D.
> Pastor Ernst Fincke
> Gustav Huhn
> Pastor Max Lackmann
> Pastor Wolfgang Lehmann

V

The autumn conference of the *Sammlung* took place in
Fürsteneck from the twenty-fifth to the twenty-eighth of
September. On the first day the sessions were attended by
Protestants only. Richard Baumann lectured on the subject, "Does God Reward Good Works?" On the following
day, our Catholic friends were present. Provost Dr. Asmussen and Professor Dr. Volk gave the introductory talks on
the subject, "Who Can Forgive Sins?" It was inevitable
that in the course of the lectures and discussions our differences in belief and practice should come clearly to the
fore. Painful as separation is in itself, these conversations
are painful also, for nothing is suppressed and there is
no attempt to avoid stepping on sensitive toes. Differences
are discussed in the minutest detail, and strange as it may
seem, it is precisely this emphasis on our differences that
brings the discussion partners closer. We know of laymen
who, having borne as much as they could, and on the verge
of giving up, nevertheless were so profoundly interested
that they continued to the very end. It cannot be denied
that the Gospel's encouragement and consolation reached
and moved us through the voices of our Catholic partners
in the dialogue. We may be sure that all genuine conversations betwen members of different Churches are a kind of
strain that must be endured, and they are only real if
they are deliberately endured.

We must thank our Catholic friends for their great pa-
tience in bearing with us Lutherans. Catholics have a clear
and unequivocal structure of beliefs, and it must seem
very strange to them when they encounter statements that
are so dynamic in themselves as to appear contradictory.
We Lutherans, however, find it difficult to conceive of a

Church that is truly alive which apparently recognizes no intellectual problems in connection with its teachings. During the last two centuries we Lutherans have thrived on problems of this kind, and the effort required to solve them, rather than on the clear, unassailable doctrines which our forefathers of the sixteenth century still enjoyed. But this is carried to such extremes that some Catholics believe that there is nothing stable in us whatever and that our Evangelical Churches will soon disappear completely. It is one of our self-appointed tasks to clarify our own position on this point and help our Catholic brethren understand how the structure of our teachings, although strangely different in many respects, nevertheless expresses a permanent requisite of the Christian religion.

Many of our friends may consider this as a very small matter. But we are taking a realistic view, and we perceive how difficult things have become and how much ground must still be covered. We do not, after all, set out on this undertaking as individuals, but as representatives. Consequently we cannot make things easy for ourselves. But even if our view is entirely realistic, it is certainly not defeatist. This was proven conclusively at the three discussion sessions in Frankfurt during the week of November 11. One Catholic and one Evangelical speaker each took up the three questions in the form of a public dialogue. The subjects were: "What makes the unity of the Churches difficult at the present time?", "How should the Church act toward the State?" and "What meaning does the Motherhood of God and the Virginity of Mary have for the Church?" The discussions were jointly sponsored by the Catholic *Volkbildungswerk,* which is an adult educational program, and by the *Sammlung.* The Provost of Frankfurt, as an official of the Evangelical Church, was informed about the meetings, and more than eight hundred people attended every session. A secular newspaper wrote, "The speakers left the impression with their audience that one can be wholly uncompromising about the truth without offending against charity." It was remarkable that the audience included all social classes and especially the eager participation of young people.

What do we expect from these meetings? We want the members of both Churches to know each other better. We want differences to be seen where they really exist and not where ignorance or skepticism on both sides would haphazardly pretend to find them. We believe that the differences should actually be *seen,* for no truth can prove its strength until it approaches us in the likeness of decision. We tried this in Frankfurt and believe that we were successful. The astonishing thing is that this approach really brings us closer together. It would be a contradiction of the truth if this were denied. The stage of coexistence has ended now and something entirely new has begun. Let us have faith that God will show us in time what this new relationship is to be.

It would be desirable if we could arrange similar meetings in other cities. Perhaps there are readers of this letter who could accomplish this. It is certainly an appropriate time, for vast numbers of Christians are actually hungering for unity, and often it is the clergy who try to prevent inter-Church discussions, and we regret that the Evangelical clergy are particularly to be blamed for this. However, it must surely be a sign of weakness when we refuse to enter into conversations with our Catholic brethren. No doubt political resentment has some part in this. We learned, for instance, and with deep regret, that Provost Grüber, commissioner of the EKiD (German Evangelical

Church in Germany) relations with the Soviet Zone government of the German Democratic Republic, had cast aspersions on Cardinal Mindszenty, placing the chief blame on him for the Hungarian uprising. We do not know whether the EKiD is willing to share responsibility for the commissioner's statements. But Provost Grüber has certainly *not* spoken in our name, or in the name of the majority of Evangelical Christians in Germany. All we can do is ask the forgiveness of our Catholic brethren for remarks of this kind. Provost Grüber ought to express the real voice of our Church, but he does not do so. When such poisonous words about Cardinal Mindszenty are uttered by a high-ranking Evangelical Church leader, our lay people are consequently involved, for it is they who must make important decisions in political and economic affairs, and must bear the burden of all that necessarily follows, both politically and ecclesiastically. As a matter of principle we ought to seriously consider the right of the laity to their own point of view regarding the relations between the Churches. In this respect, there should be fewer obstacles for Protestants than for Catholics. We believe that laymen were also included in the saying, *"And they shall all be taught of God"* (Jn. 6:45). Lay people can be as mistaken as theologians, of course, but the theologians cannot wholly dispense with the voice of the laity. Therefore we must encourage laymen to express their opinions far more freely than in the past.

This is of special significance in regard to a matter that has been on all our minds for a long time. Our friends know that the Württemberg pastor, Richard Baumann, was suspended from his office and deprived of his title for teaching "heresy." Baumann, as minister and as an interpreter of Holy Scripture, had spoken of Christ's promise in a way that was novel to Protestants. He said that Christ wanted to build His Church on St. Peter, the Rock. A great deal remains to be said about this case, especially in regard to the method used in the ecclesiastical proceedings against Baumann. We need only compare the Württemberg law, which was the basis of Pastor Baumann's conviction, with the doctrinal system of the Lutheran Churches in Germany, to perceive at first glance that the two methods orginate from wholly different interpretations of law and creed.

Professor D. Brunner of Heidelberg, whose point of view is very close to our own, has written an article that is essentially devoted to the Richard Baumann affair. This article is of special significance because the author is one of the best-known Lutheran theologians of our day. We regret that Professor Brunner agrees with the Württemberg High Consistory without giving due consideration to the details of the trial procedure. Nor can we understand why this particular case, a controversy regarding the papacy, should be singled out when there is certainly no shortage of real heresies among us. Can we talk about the Baumann case while keeping complete silence about all the other Protestant heresies that are rampant today? We need only think how greatly our lay people are disturbed regarding the teachings of Bultmann and his followers, which are now being disseminated from our pulpits and practiced on our altars! We may well wonder how this can result in better relations between the Churches.

Consistently with his reputation, Professor Brunner does not deal with Baumann's case in a merely negative way. He also tries to answer the question which the papacy poses for us all. In this respect, he develops the teaching about the bishoprics and their relations with each other, and with the papacy too, which is deserving of serious attention. His comments are like those which at one time were perhaps expressive of a Catholic point of view concerning the office of the papacy, while we on the Evangelical side have been considering the papacy in a very different light. Much as we regret the abrupt dismissal of the Baumann case by Professor Brunner, we are nevertheless grateful, for the sake of our work, that a Lutheran theologian has given such serious thought to a question that we have been stressing with persistent emphasis. We feel that this must be regarded as a truly remarkable advance.

We must express the same appreciation of the thoughtfulness and serious attention devoted to relations with the Roman Catholic Church during the Lutheran Bishops' Conference in Hanover in their session at the end of November. Our friends will have learned from both press and radio reports that "the efforts of various groups and individuals within the German Evangelical Church to approach the Roman theology" were also given a fair hearing. "The conference requested the Theological Committee to devote particular effort to these tasks in the near future. Bishop D. Dietzfelbinger, of Bavaria, was elected as commissioner of the United Church for these matters." We all wish him God's blessing in his work.

Friends of the *Sammlung* will join us in thanking God that the number of those who are unhappy about our separation from the historic Mother Church of the West is steadily increasing. Our theological study, our discussions and meetings, (several of us were in Rome this fall for private, informative visits) and last but not least the historical developments in the secular world during the past few months have confirmed our belief that the gospel of Jesus Christ in itself can no longer give us any peace while disunity continues. Perhaps the coming of the Lord is also being heralded through these "signs of the times."

We say to our friends, therefore, in the words of the Introit of both Churches for the Second Sunday in Advent, *People of Sion, behold the Lord shall come to save the nations; and the Lord shall make the glory of His voice to be heard in the joy of your heart. Give ear, O Thou that rulest Israel: Thou that leadest Joseph like a sheep.*

Advent, 1956

> Dr. Hans Asmussen, D.D.
> Gustav Huhn
> Pastor Ernst Fincke
> Pastor Max Lackmann
> Pastor Wolfgang Lehmann

VI

The following letter was sent to the Sammlung leaders by Protestants of the Evangelical Church in Communist East Germany.

Dear Brethren:

The theological and secular questions which affect the Churches in the German Democratic Republic (under Communist control) cannot be considered apart from the daily disputes with the totalitarian Communist State in which we live. Internal questions of an ecclesiastical kind which confront us because of the historical development of Reformation teachings and the very character of the Church itself, also derive their special urgency from this present struggle. We cannot for a moment forget that the existence of all Christian Churches in our country is now seriously threatened, and that Communism, both in principle and in practice has placed the Churches in a condition of real privation. Consequently we are all bound by a common Christian responsibility. In this struggle of faith we meet anew as brethren, and we are ready and determined to preserve and deepen our communion in Christ above and beyond the companionship we share in this struggle. But this also means that we are hindered by the schism between the Churches which affects the solution of all the practical ecclesiastical problems. We pray that this situation may soon be overcome. We are therefore earnestly trying to help one another and we are striving to be rid of the offensive attitudes that were certainly never necessary for the sake of the gospel's truth as we understand it. For this reason we seek a better understanding of the devotion of our Catholic brethren and we rejoice over all the blessings that Our Lord has bestowed upon their Church. In this harmony of faith we are more willing than were our forefathers to listen and learn from each other and to make fruitful our common spiritual heritage for the life and struggle of the Church today.

When our Bishop, in an hour of serious difficulty, addressed a pastoral letter to his flock, he was faced with the question of issuing an order or merely requesting that the letter be read aloud from every pulpit. He decided in favor of making a request, in order to avoid giving the impression of exercising any force, however lawful. About half of the pastors complied and the letter was read aloud to their congregations. In view of the customary individualism prevalent in Evangelical churches, this may seem like astonishing unanimity. But it is precisely in this respect that a need becomes apparent which has been observed and noted by the State and Party very closely. The real need, however, lies much deeper. What can be said about the Evangelical episcopal office and its authority? What is the relationship between this office and the unity of the Church, especially in times of persecution? It is significant that similar pastoral letters of Catholic bishops were read by all Catholic priests with complete unanimity. We may well ask what is the reason for this difference, and how the remedy may be found for such a deficiency among us.

Another problem that troubles us is the matter of the Church's ministry. We have a serious shortage of ministers, and as far as we can foresee, this situation will become worse as the years go by. Before long only half of our existing rectories will be occupied by ministers who have been trained in theology and ordained for this life and work. Is it right to persuade laymen in the parish churches to abandon their own occupations in order to receive seminary training for ordination and appointment as *preachers?* We need to consider carefully the relationship between the ministry of preaching and that of the pastor. Are we permitted to put the care of a parish, including the administration of the sacraments, in the hands of specially qualified laymen? We must give serious thought to the services now being performed by laymen in our Evangelical churches. There have been new developments in this situation during the past few years, and we must now face the fact that the number of active lay people who are willing and able to assume parochial duties has sharply diminished. There are many ministers who are simply overwhelmed by the burdens of preaching and the care of souls because they cannot cope with these responsibilities adequately. But this is only one aspect of the problem. In other respects an even more urgent question confronts us in regard to the relationship between the common priesthood of the laity and the ordained ministry of the Church. This must be clarified by way of example. During the Frankfurt Congress of the German Evangelical Church the question of auricular confession was one of the topics under consideration and was discussed with eager participation by the audience. The use of confession has been allowed among us, with specially appointed members of the Church, including both clergy and laity, having authority in this matter, but who really possesses Our Lord's command and authority to hear confessions and grant absolution? Confession is not a generally accepted sacrament in Evangelical Churches, and until recently it was all but unknown. Whenever it is desired now it is almost always because of special circumstances, as in times of oppression, or when there is an obligation to be secretive during investigative activities of the police. What about the Seal of the Confessional? The minister is bound to absolute silence by his vow of ordination. But who has dispensed the layman from the vow of silence if he can serve the needs of his brethren by virtue of the common priesthood of the laity? Or has anyone bound the layman to silence also? And who enforces the keeping of such a vow? It should not be surprising if the question of ordination, i.e., the question of the *ordo,* is brought up again in regard to the matter of confession as it concerns both the ministers and the laity of our Church.

We Lutherans like to call our Church the *Church of the Word.* We are proud of our preaching ministry. Nevertheless, it is an open secret among us that our sermons are largely lacking in real spiritual authority and that our congregations are hungering for prayer and the sacraments. We are now trying to celebrate the Lord's Supper more frequently in our churches, and as far as possible we hold a service once a month with this rite included. The experience has taught us that the number of communicants will increase steadily, but the more often that holy communion is administered and received among us the more need there is to consider the divine gift we receive in this sacrament. What can we say about communion with Our Lord enthroned in this sacrament? Is the Lord's Supper nothing more than the *visible word?* Or is it truly a sacramental presence and communion with the Lord who was crucified for us? We must ask ourselves to what extent we believe in the presence of Christ in the bread and wine. Are we sure of these beliefs and do they give us joy? It is difficult to understand the apathy and indifference of Evangelical Christians in regard to this gift of their Lord. Perhaps it is the result of our shortening the celebration of the Eucharist as compared with the full liturgy of the ancient Church and the unbroken liturgical traditions of the Roman Catholic and Eastern Orthodox Churches in their celebration of the Mass. What do we really believe about the Sacrifice of the Mass? Can we say that the Roman Mass is a "horrible idolatry" as the Reformers declared? Or is it an authentic celebration of the holy Eucharist? In this connection let us return once more to the question of the Ministry. We must decide who rightly possesses Christ's authority to administer the sacrament of the altar. We must think about the ministry of the priest in regard to the Sacrifice of the Mass. It is possible that indifference to the Lord's Supper in Evangelical Churches, and our apparent helplessness in trying to revive love and reverence for the sacrament of the altar, may be due to Evangelical teaching about this sacrament, or perhaps it is because the priestly ministry was changed into a mere *ministerium verbi divini,* a simple preaching ministry. We mention this question because in the midst of the Church's present distress and the temptations that have consequently arisen, we need the fullness of the divine gift of mercy through the authority of the priestly ministry.

These questions are not undisputed even in our troubled Church. Considerable theological objection is raised against liturgical reforms and against the contemporary efforts to overcome the differences between the various Churches. There are even serious objections against the common front of opposition to Communism, especially if the Catholic Church is included. While many Evangelical pastors and lay people gratefully read the sermons and pastoral letters of Catholic bishops, and the papal encyclicals also, and listen to them on the radio as well, there are theologians and Church leaders who are still repeating the accusations of the Reformation, telling us that the pope is the Anti-Christ and the Catholic Church is the synagogue of Satan! Those who try, in a brotherly manner, to overcome ecclesiastical schisms are accused and put on trial for their efforts. As a matter of fact, the sincerity and genuineness of their struggle against godless materialism and the Communist State, and their refusal to regard the Roman Church as a fanatical and fascist enemy, has placed them all under suspicion. This has caused great distress among us and perhaps, dear members of the *Sammlung,* you can now understand why some of us follow your achievements with a burning heart. We pray with you for the unity of all holy Churches and we support every endeavor to foster serious ecumenical discussions with all Churches, and above all with the Catholic Church, from which we are separated in schism.

This letter from the Church in the German Democratic Republic (of the Soviet area) is shared with our friends in the hope that they may clearly see that the hopes of the Sammlung and its aims are in accordance with the real need of the Church.

Pre-Lent, 1957

> Dr. Hans Asmussen, D.D.
> Gustav Huhn
> Pastor Ernst Fincke
> Pastor Max Lackmann
> Pastor Wolfgang Lehmann

VII

With this letter we are discontinuing the circular letters for the present. This does not mean that we have lost interest in the work which was undertaken, or that we have lost faith that we are engaged in a worthy cause. Nor have we reason to suppose that our message will no longer be given a hearing. However, if we no longer use the circular letters, it is only because a particular kind of activity serves a purpose for a limited period of time, and for various reasons we have decided to pursue our work in a different way.

In the theses that follow we are presenting a summary of what we consider important in our undertaking thus far. We expect to hear from many readers complaining that the contents of this letter are too difficult for them or too condensed. The subject matter is indeed very difficult, and the wording has required careful phrasing, for it is not given to men to write of spiritual matters in a manner that is easy to grasp and readily understandable. Anyone who attempts to discuss matters of this kind must necessarily express himself as God allows him to speak, and will hope that some day his readers will feel that he is speaking their language. With this purpose in mind, we are planning to enlarge upon the subject of these theses in a small book, and this will be undertaken immediately. We want to help all those who are concerned about the continued existence of our Church, the salvation of souls and the unity of Christendom.

What have we really accomplished?

It could be said in reply, "Little enough!" As a matter of fact, except for members of the *Michaelsbruderschaft*,[1] there has been no desire on the part of Protestants to enter into discussions with us apart from certain individuals who accepted our invitation. If our judgment of what has happened is only superficial, then we must admit that we are not satisfied with the results of our endeavors. On the other hand, we know that the questions brought up in our circular letters have become subjects of discussion throughout the Church, and this can be attributed to our efforts. For the past year the Catholic Question has been under consideration among bishops, theologians and other leaders of the Church to a surprising degree, even though it has been customary for many years to refuse any serious consideration of the Roman Catholic Church for political and theological reasons. We feel that our success in this respect is not without importance. Needless to say, we have been accused of "Catholic" tendencies and consequently it was particularly easy for others to avoid discussions with us or to boycott us. Some "Protestants" regard "Catholic tendencies" as something considerably worse

---

[1] A Protestant society dedicated to the restoration of the liturgy, and the revival of other catholic beliefs and practices.

than attitudes that are not Christian at all. There are still many "Protestants" in political or intellectual circles who would rather be seen with non-Christians than with Roman Catholics. But we will accept the reproach and admit to Catholic tendencies. It becomes increasingly apparent that the reproach requires a decision from us which can be regarded as *the* decision of our time. We are convinced that *only that which is universally Christian is Christian at all*. That which is *catholic* is Christian. Whatever is merely partial or local is not Christian. The quest for authentic catholicity is the mission of our era. One example may clarify this statement. Everyone knows that the Lutheran churches in Germany are trying to restore a liturgical service that can claim to be universal, i.e., catholic. It is commonly assumed that this can be accomplished only by a return to those forms of divine service that were used by Martin Luther and his disciples. It is clearly recognized that the Lord's Supper should be included in the divine service again and no longer remain as an unorganic appendage. However, it is no mere coincidence that well-known "Protestants" even suspect these efforts of the Lutheran Church as questionable Catholicizing tendencies. This is precisely where those who want to recover all that is universally Christian distinguish themselves from others who are satisfied with the partial and incomplete.

It may, of course, be doubted whether the divine service celebrated among us during the Reformation era was actually the rite that was universally Christian, the catholic liturgy. The Church will have to investigate this question very thoroughly. However, we can no longer seriously doubt that whatever is universally Christian should be the deciding factor for us. Only the universally

Christian is true. That is why we hope, in the following theses, to arouse interest and discussion, in language that is understandable to Protestants, regarding the nature of universal Christian truths. We believe that this criterion is so important that we are even inquiring about certain aspects of Roman Catholicism to determine whether these can really be understood and accepted as "catholic" in this sense. In the light of this principle, we do not have "Catholic tendencies." We have a passion for catholicity. And this belongs in the Christian faith.

Fürsteneck (Hesse), May 16, 1957

> Dr. Hans Asmussen, D.D.
> Gustav Huhn
> Pastor Ernst Fincke
> Pastor Max Lackmann
> Richard Baumann
> Pastor Wolfgang Lehmann

EVANGELICAL AFFIRMATIONS
OF CATHOLIC TRUTHS

1. The whole Word of God

In the course of our Church's history a number of *catholic truths* have been lost which must be recovered. Catholic truths are universal truths of Christendom and the Church cannot obediently and authoritatively carry out her mandate to maintain the truth of the Gospel and the unity of Christendom without them.

We Lutherans claim to be the Church of the Word, but it becomes ever more apparent that we often place limitations upon the Word of God in order to prevent any contradiction of our particular ecclesiastical principles. The loss of essential Catholic truths leads to the isolation and exaggeration of other truths of the Christian faith, and this results in the divisions which rend the Body of Christ asunder and weaken the message of the Gospel. We are presenting an outline of the catholic truths which we must all again profess if we really wish to be the Church of the New Testament and the Apostles' Creed, and if we are sincere in our desire to serve the cause of the unity of the one catholic and apostolic Church.

2. The Incarnation of the Word and the Christian mysteries of faith

The Word became flesh. Salvation comes to man and to every living creature from above, and not from creation or from human effort. Proportionate to its coming, however, the saving *Word* itself becomes *flesh,* that is to say, it takes creation and human nature, deprived of salvation since the Fall, and elevates them to the service of God.

It is a catholic truth that the act of salvation by the Son of God incarnate is most certainly unique, but it occurs just as certainly in the *always* of the present. The presence of Christ's act of salvation is continued in His mysteries, the divine miracles of intervention in response to faith. These are His Word and His sacraments.

It is a catholic truth that a divine mystery can be believed only through enlightenment by the Holy Spirit.

The Christian mysteries become operative through the power of the incarnation of the Son of God in such a way that God uses a particular human act of divine worship, considered integrally, including both the ministry of the word and the administration of the sacraments, and makes this act His own, blessing it in order that it may become a mystery of faith. The loss of a catholic truth is indicated whenever the correspondence of divine and human acts in the sacramental mysteries is disregarded. Anyone who claims that God alone is acting in these mysteries proves by this very statement that he has not passed beyond the initial stage of the saving act of God, although he ought to be able to explain the whole process intelligently.

3. Grace and Freedom

It is a catholic truth that the individual attains salvation only in the measure that he is fashioned anew in the image of Christ. Christians are born again as members of Christ independent of the will of the flesh or of man. They die His death and will be resurrected to share His life. The

Christian life can never be dissociated from the birth, death, and resurrection of Christ.

The formulation of this question in terms of man's *free will* should be reconsidered, for this concept is derived from non-Christian philosophy. We can neither maintain the self-sufficiency of man, separated from God, as the deciding factor, nor can we claim, in the philosophical manner, a complete helplessness behind which our own self-willed decisions are concealed. The mystery of faith consists rather in God's transformation of the unwilling into the willing. The individual's way to faith can be pointed out in no other way than by our showing, as far as possible, how resisting persons can become cooperative.

It is also a catholic truth that we are saved by grace alone, just as it is a Evangelical truth that God does not save us without our cooperation. The apparent contradiction contained in this statement can be surmounted when we realize that God, in leading us to salvation, cannot be understood in terms of the categories of rational causality concepts. It is therefore necessary that we give scriptural evidence that God rewards every good deed of believers and unbelievers both in time and eternity. This truth, however, does not contradict the doctrine that salvation is a gift.

4. The Mystery of the Church

The *WORD* made flesh, the crucified and risen Lord, continues His life and work in the life and work of His Body, the Church. For this reason, and in relation to Christ, the Church is called a *mysterium* in the New Testament, because it is not merely a community of hearers of the Word, but simultaneously one with the *WORD* incarnate, "of his flesh and of his bones" (Ephesians 5:30). Therefore the Church is not only spiritual and invisible but also corporeal and visible, even in regard to its lawful authority, instituted by God. The offices and services of the Church are the *joints* of this Body (Ephesians 4:16). It is a loss of a catholic truth when a large body which calls itself a *Church* no longer conceives of itself as a mystery and no longer realizes that it is inseparably one with the primal sacrament which is Christ. Consequently it is erroneous to suppose that we can perceive the Church as a spiritual mystery when we are regarding her visible appearance exclusively and deliberately ignoring her sacramental character also. Even though it be the will of God that we *see* the Church, we do not see her as the *Body of Christ,* for however true it may be that God wills that only through faith can the Church be recognized as the Body of Christ, we know that faith can acknowledge only what is seen with earthly vision.

5. The Relationship of the Head to the Body

Christ is the *Head* of the Church, her Lord, and the source of her life. At the same time, the Church is His *Body,* constituting together with Himself the one and entire Christ (I Cor. 12:12). The Church lives by the sacrifice of Christ, once offered, and yet this sacrifice for ourselves and for the world is not all that it ought to be and might be, for it requires all the many co-sacrifices and co-sufferings of His Body the Church (Col. 1:24).

Christ alone is the king and the priest who governs and reconciles all things, yet He permits the Church to share in this royal and sacerdotal ministry (Apocalypse 5:10). Members of the Church participate partly in a free and

informal manner, while some are specially chosen for hierarchical positions, high and low, in diverse kinds of ecclesiastical functions.

Christ is the only Teacher who instructs the Church
through the Word, according as this was recorded by the
Apostles; however, His Word becomes *flesh* even in the
Church's historical decisions and in the formulation of
her dogmas and her life. Consequently, the word of the
Church also participates in the authority of her Master.
The unity of Christ with His Church, and the definite dis-
tinction between them, must both be kept clearly in mind.
It is a loss of a catholic truth to see only *one* side of this
relationship.

6. The Sacrifice of Christ and the Sacrifice of the Church

The reconciling sacrifice of Christ is an act which sur-
passes understanding. It was executed in the depth of His
loving heart, in the bloody crucifixion, and in His entire
passage through the world to His Father. The victim is
the High Priest for all eternity. He re-presents His sacrifice
in the sacraments of the Church, especially in the holy
Eucharist, and receives into Himself the living sacrifices
of all Christians. It is not only the Person of Christ who
is present in the Eucharistic rite, but also the entire act of
His sacrifice. But none of this occurs without the cooperation of the Church, and more especially the priests and
other servants of the altar who administer the sacrament.
This is why Christian worship is a sacrifice in a complete
and proper sense of the term. The expiatory sacrifice of
Christ and the eucharistic sacrifice of the Church are not
wholly separate from each other, but rather the thanksgiving and prayer and expiatory self-sacrifice of Christ are

one with the thanksgiving, prayer and expiatory self-giving of the Church. The expiatory sacrifices of Christians do not diminish the glory of Christ but rather increase it.

7. The Church and the Apostolic Succession of Bishops

The Church and her mysteries, which we call sacraments, are closely related. Special circumstances may make the use of "private sacraments" necessary in our faith, but cannot take the place of ecclesiastical authority. It is a loss of an essential catholic truth if preaching of the Word is too freely undertaken. Preaching should be subject to the same careful supervision as the administration of the sacraments, with proper authorization. This must be a visible and legal authority and yet also supernaturally operative and efficacious. Renunciation of a clear conception of authority was and is the principal cause of the divisions of Christendom. It is a matter for all Christians to decide whether Ordination is more efficacious in our Churches than a simple administrative authorization.

Our Lord chose the twelve Apostles for a wholly new, Christlike, and priestly vocation, participating in His own authority. He blessed them in this calling, and to some He gave pre-eminence, even as He chose one of them for a position of leadership. In the course of the apostolic era this basic structure developed into a hierarchy of bishops, priests and deacons. According to this original hierarchical order they were not merely functionaries of a Church or a community, but were specially endowed by the ascended Lord for the transmission of the general and the particular priesthood of the New Covenant. They are not to act autocratically, for they are only set apart for particular functions within the wider, general ministry of the Church.

However, the gradation shows that all baptized persons, in the broadest sense, participate in this ministry. All vocations are functions, although on essentially different levels, of the one ministry of the royal priesthood of the Church. It is especially necessary that the Church's ministry, patterned after the relationship between Christ and the Apostles, be inseparably associated with a person who has been specially consecrated for the office. The transmission of the general priesthood which originates with Baptism imparts a new life and is inalienable. The same may be said regarding the special priesthood of the ministry which is transmitted by a holder of the apostolic office who has authority to ordain.

The calling of a woman to the ministry destroys the sacramental character of the office which was meant to be a representation of the heavenly bridegroom of the Church. Just as milk is inconceivable as a substitute for wine in the Eucharist for consecration as Christ's blood, it is likewise unthinkable that a member of the female sex should be ordained as a minister representing Christ. However, the calling of women to other offices in the Church is not considered questionable on this account.

8. The Ministry and Ordination

It is a lost catholic truth that the priesthood belongs to the Church for the sake of the sacramental character of the Church. How else could the succession of Christ, the High Priest, be continued? It is a facile evasion to say that the "priesthood of all believers" prevails throughout the whole Church everywhere, and consequently no priests are necessary. The catholic truth that Christians are a priestly people categorically requires an explanation of the nature and scope of priestly functions and clear indication of the particular Christians who are authorized and ordained to exercise these special functions as successors of Christ.

It is a catholic truth that Confirmation, although not yet formally defined as such, is the authorization for the general priesthood of all the faithful, but something more is needed beyond Confirmation to ensure the efficacy of the sacraments. The authorization for priestly service, to which the preaching of the Word also belongs, according to the New Testament, is a mystery and a sacrament in itself. Christ imparts grace and the charismatic character of the ministry Himself through the instrumentality of consecrated servants of the Church.

The sacrament of Ordination could only be conferred by the Apostles or those who were authorized by them. Ever since the functional division of the priestly ministry in the early Church, under the guidance of the Holy Spirit, the authority of Ordination has belonged to the bishops only. Episcopal transmission of the priestly ministry is the sacramental sign willed by God whereby the temporal and spatial unity of the Church and her ministry finds expression.

9. One Head of the Church

It is a catholic truth that the Church of Christ on earth has, and should have, but *one* head. Jesus said to the Apostles collectively, "He that heareth you, heareth me" (Lk. 10:16). But He also bestowed His supreme pastoral ministry on one particular Apostle and called him *the Rock* (Peter), who would be the foundation stone of the Church and her protection against the gates of hell (Jn. 21:15 ff; Jn. 1:42; Mt. 16:18). It is unthinkable that the commis-

sioning of the many would continue while the pastoral
ministry of the one should cease. Biblical testimony confronts the Evangelical ecumenical movement with the
need to determine the significance of this supreme pastoral
office for all Christians. If the bishop of Rome claims to
hold this office as St. Peter's successor, in accordance with
ancient ecclesiastical tradition, then Evangelical Christianity can no longer evade the issue of considering the
papal claims in the light of biblical revelation which
clearly indicates the special office of St. Peter.

If we give our assent to the divine urgency of this problem, it does not mean that we could ever sanction the particular development of this authority in certain periods
of history when it had deteriorated into a worldly and un-
christian domination over conscience. Nor can we neglect
the question, still undecided, of the re-establishment of
this primatial authority in a proper relationship to the
authority that belongs to all bishops and their particular
churches. It is, however, a serious error to reject the idea
of *one* head of the universal Church on earth.

10. Church, Scripture and Tradition

It is a catholic truth, accepted throughout the whole
Church everywhere, that the individual finds his true self
only within the fellowship of the Church. It is consequently wrong not to help the individual find self-fulfill-
ment within the Church, just as it is an error to wish to
attain salvation by one's own efforts alone, apart from the
living community of the Church. A healthy life of faith
is only possible if the Church itself lives in communion
with the faithful and the hierarchy of all times and all
places. It is a catholic truth that a generation which wants

to be free of feelings of guilt, must think ecumenically. The individual will suffer spiritual damage if the Church, of which he is a member, is no longer in communion with the Christians of all times, all peoples and all places. It is a catholic truth that we must hold fast to that *"which everywhere and at all times has been believed by all men"* (Vincent of Lerins).

The Word of God was recorded in the New Testament, a unique, inspired document of the primitive Church, in order to guide and accompany the Church in her long passage through history, and to conserve and transmit this record in its exact and apostolic form. This Word, through the Holy Spirit, is continually unfolded through history also as tradition, whether in the dynamic form of spiritual life or in the fixed form of ecclesiastical doctrine, liturgy or canon law. These developments do not occur by decision of the Church, however, for the Church cannot arbitrarily proclaim dogmas or devise regulations that go beyond the requirements of human nature, for she is bound to the great moments of history chosen by the Holy Spirit. The Word of Christ is determinative for the decisions and proclamations of these moments and the Church is necessarily committed to His Word.

It is a fallacy to think that the absolute subordination of the Church to the revealed Word of God in Holy Scripture is weakened or even impeded by being bound to the tradition of the Church. Absolute subordination to the revealed Word of God only becomes possible in full measure through proper commitment to the tradition of the Church.

The current rediscovery of *catholic truths* in Holy Scripture signifies that Reformation Christianity is called by the Holy Spirit to a new and positive relationship with the Roman Catholic Church. The rediscovered catholic truths of the Gospel had already been clearly vindicated as divine truths by pre-Reformation Christianity. It is inconceivable that Evangelical Churches could recover these catholic truths and yet fail to seek reunion with the historic Eastern and Western Churches which have always, under the guidance of the Holy Spirit, held fast to them.

11. The Teaching Ministry

It is a loss of a catholic truth if a bishop neither wishes nor is allowed to exercise his teaching ministry, or if he does not permit anything to be taught by his authority regarding the common belief and practice of Christians who are "all taught by God." The bishop is not merely an administrator with the title of *bishop,* but is the teacher of his diocese and the one person on whom the preservation of unity with all other bishoprics must depend.

The layman is not merely the object of ecclesiastical activity. In a very real sense he is also the subject. When the people have a voice in the selection of their bishop by acclamation, as for example when they chose St. Ambrose in the fourth century, something of the mystery of Christ and of His Church is realized.

12. The Communion of Saints

It is a sign of healthy spiritual life if the relationship between the Church and departed Christians is not merely historical, but based upon a belief that all those who are waiting and beseeching, praying and worshipping, in the immediate presence of God are also participating in the fellowship of the Church Militant here on earth. This association of the earthly and the heavenly Church has a biblical basis. In the services of the Church we show forth the everlasting communion of all the saints. The Eucharistic Communion of the Body and Blood of Christ, especially, unites all the saints in heaven and on earth.

MAX LACKMANN

THE CALL OF EVANGELICAL CHRISTIANITY TO CATHOLIC FULFILLMENT

I

In the Apostles' Creed the Church voices belief in "the holy Catholic Church." The Nicene Creed declares more fully, "I believe in . . . one, holy, Catholic and Apostolic Church." As a rule, most Evangelical Christians no longer realize that the word *catholic* properly belongs in the creed of the Church. In their present-day religious services and ecclesiastical instruction this word is simply omitted, and the terms *universal* or *Christian* are used instead. *Catholic* has become a denominational designation for Christians who are subject to papal jurisdiction. The Evangelical Protestant is apparently unwilling to be Catholic in any sense of the term. Even Evangelical church leaders and well-known theologians are interested in the catholicity of the Church in a merely incidental way or, in some cases, not at all. During the first World War, in the city of Munich, the great Lutheran churchman, Hermann Bezzel, preached a series of doctrinal sermons on the Apostles' Creed.[1] The "all-inclusive" Church (as Bezzel renders the term Catholic), was mentioned very briefly, while all other articles of the creed were explained quite thoroughly in their full biblical significance. Readers of the doctrinal

1 Hermann Bezzel, *Die 3 Glaubensartikel in Katechismusstunden*, 1925.

66

manuals of Paul Althaus and Werner Elert find that the subject is still receiving the same kind of treatment today. But Karl Barth, in his most recent book, *Kirkliche Dogmatik,* has now at least made a beginning in his deliberate efforts to end the traditional Evangelical contempt for the word *Catholic.* "The renunciation of this term is really impossible. A Church is Catholic or it is not a Church." [2] Barth then tries, in his own way, to restore to Protestant belief the full significance of the word *Catholic* in the Christian creed. When we read the *Loci theologici* of Johann Gerhard,[3] a standard doctrinal work of Lutheran orthodoxy of the seventeenth century, we see how persuasively the Evangelical theologian defines the catholicity of the Church in various respects, and we are readily convinced that our own indifference to the Catholic character of the Church becomes "an indication of the greatest thoughtlessness and weakness." [4]

The distinguishing mark of the Church as *Catholic* is evidently derived from those who first heard and accepted the message of revelation, and likewise from ecclesiastical dogma which is essential for all of us because of the great worth of truth and salvation. In the year 110 A.D., when "the earth was still warm with Christ's blood" (St. Jerome), the bishop and martyr Ignatius wrote to a Christian community while traveling to Rome, "Where Jesus Christ may be, there also is the Catholic Church." [5] Forty-seven years later, an eye-witness of the martyrdom of blessed Polycarp reported to the "Church of God in Philomelium

2 Karl Barth, *Kirchliche Dogmatik* IV, 1, 1953, p. 784 ff.

3 Johann Gerhard, *Loci theologici,* ed. Fr. Frank (1885), Vol. 5, Locus 22, p. 277.

4 Karl Barth, *op. cit.,* p. 784.

5 Letter to the Church of Smyrna, *Die Apostolischen Väter,* ed. K. Bihlmeyer, 1924, p. 108, 20.

and all communities of the Catholic Church everywhere." [6]
We are told that the blessed martyr had rejoiced in the
communion of all the saints "with Our Lord Jesus Christ,
the redeemer of our souls, the guardian of our bodies, the
shepherd of the Catholic Church throughout the world." [7]
Thirty years afterwards, in a famous commentary on New
Testament writings,[8] we read of the "Catholic Church"
several times, which the authors had in mind even when
they were writing to some local congregation or a particular individual. Probably as early as the third century
a form of the Apostles' Creed, as it is commonly called,
and very similar to the creed of the Roman Church, was
used in a Coptic liturgy in Egypt; the people professed
their faith "in the resurrection of the body in the holy
Catholic Church." [9] A hundred years later the expression
"holy Catholic and Apostolic Church" was heard in the
official Credo of the whole Christian world. The Athanasian Creed (between 425 and 600 A.D.), one of the three
creeds of the ancient Church, which is binding upon
Evangelical Christianity also, could even begin with the
severe formula, "Whosoever will be saved, before all
things it is necessary that he hold the Catholic Faith,
which faith except everyone do keep whole and undefiled,
without doubt he shall perish everlastingly." [10]

Deliberate renunciation of life in the "Catholic"
Church, and of the "Catholic" faith, would consequently
exclude us from communion with the redeeming God,
just as certainly as would happen if we were to delete the

6 *Op. cit.*, p. 120, Martyrdom of Bl. Polycarp.

7 *Op. cit.*, p. 130, 20.

8 Muratorian Canon in H. Lietzmann's *Kleine Texte,* 1902.

9 Denzinger, *Enchiridion Symbolorum,* 1952, No. 1.

10 *Bekenntnisschriften der Evangelisch-lutherischen Kirche,* 1930, Vol.
1, p. 28.

little word *holy* or the expression *became man* from other articles of the creed. We are either Catholic Christians or we are not Christians at all. There is no third possibility.

The word *Catholic* must therefore denote a most important aspect of revealed truth in regard to both the faith and the Church. Efforts to make translations of the term that are linguistically accurate, as for instance the use of *universal* or *all-inclusive,* refer only to the external wording and do not lead to an understanding of the inner meaning which appertains to Christ and the Holy Spirit. Nobody will grasp the real inner meaning of the words *apostolic* and *sacrament* if there is merely an attempt to understand them in their root meaning, in a philosophical and rational manner, instead of the particular meaning they acquired in the common life of the Church which adopted and transmitted these terms as expressions of authentic experiences in the practice of the Christian religion. Nevertheless, the word *Catholic* in the creed has now become quite meaningless or merely optional for all those who do not accept the full significance of this word derived from the Christian experience of the historic Church of the ages.

There is no mention of the *Catholic Church* in the New Testament, nor will we find such words as sacrament, Mass, confession or ordination. It can be shown, however, that the full meaning of *Catholic* is simply a development of the original concept of divine salvation and of Christ and His Church in the world, and that is a sufficient basis for our use of the term. What the Church of Jesus Christ learns, believes, professes and teaches as dogma when she conceives of herself as the Catholic Church can be set forth under five aspects.

1. *The Church is called Catholic* in contradistinction
to the People of God of the ancient covenant who were
confined to the Israelite nation in their land of Palestine
and to the adherents of the Temple in Jerusalem. "In
Judea is God known: his name is great in Israel" (Ps. 76:1
in the King James version or Ps. 75:1 in the Douay Bible).
"The Lord hath said it, whose fire is in Sion, and his
furnace in Jerusalem" (Isaias 31:9). However, in the New
Covenant there is the fulfillment of the prophetical promise that in Abraham's seed, i.e., in Christ, all peoples will
be blessed and will be gathered together in the New Jerusalem (Genesis 12:3; Isaias 2:2 ff.). To the Messias the
promise was made, "I will give thee the Gentiles for thy
inheritance, and the utmost parts of the earth for thy possession" (Ps. 2:8). To His Name a clean oblation is offered
and "in every place" there is sacrifice (Mal. 1:11). The
baptismal command of Jesus and the commissioning of the
Apostles as missionaries, inaugurated the new "Catholicity" embracing the whole world with all its languages,
religions, races and nations, and pointed to the fulfillment
of the Church's destiny: "Going therefore, teach ye all
nations: baptizing them. . . ." (Mt. 28:19), "and you shall
be witnesses unto me . . . even to the uttermost part of
the earth" (Acts 1:8). The People of Christ therefore exist
simultaneously either as national or local churches, and in
relation to Christ, as the one Catholic Church of all places,
everywhere identical, comprising all nations, races, countries and cultures. At the present time the Evangelical
"Churches" are commonly using the word *ecumenical* in
reference to this aspect of Catholicity. Karl Barth would
certainly be right if he acknowledged responsibility for
this substitution and also for the absurd but emotion-

charged contrasting of the terms Catholic and Protestant in our modern Protestant usage of these words.[11]

2. *The Church is called Catholic* because all the particular Christian communities everywhere on earth which have a right to be considered as "churches," together with all their individual members, comprise one "holy temple in the Lord" (Eph. 2:21) as the one, "all-inclusive" Catholic Church of the whole world. As early as the time of the Apostles the Jewish Christian church in Jerusalem and the Gentile churches in Antioch, Asia Minor and Greece were fully aware of their membership in the one "Catholic" fold of the one Shepherd (Jn. 10:16). In the second century the Church had already designated the first and second epistles of Peter and the epistle of James as "Catholic Epistles" because they were addressed to "the strangers dispersed" everywhere, and "to them that have obtained equal faith with us" and to the "twelve tribes which are scattered abroad." It was also because they were, in certain respects, intended for the whole Church generally, that is to say, the Catholic Church.

The Church as a whole, in its historic, visible, growing and maturing form (and not merely as an object of faith), an organism guided by the Holy Spirit, and from its very beginnings as the primitive Christian community in Jerusalem, became the example and norm for all spiritual formation and development of particular parts and members, whether as individual Christians or local congregations (Acts 8:5-25). For the *whole* includes the multiplicity of all its parts and members. Moreover, every local church derives its rights and functions as a "habitation of the Lord" in order that the whole Body of Christ may exist, and only for this reason. On the other hand, however,

11 *Op. cit.,* p. 785.

every local or national Church represents the whole Catholic Church because it functions as an integral part of the whole Body of Christ of all times, all places and all peoples. A congregation in Sweden, a church in Australia, is always first and foremost the Church of Christ if it lives its spiritual life as a subordinate member of the *whole* Catholic and Apostolic Church. We possess Christ and the Holy Spirit, as individuals and as churches, only as members incorporate of His whole Body.

3. *The Church is called Catholic* because the orthodox and redemptive faith is the only "catholic" faith, i.e. this faith alone proceeds from the concordant experience in belief, the common credal witness and profession of faith of devout and faithful members of the Catholic Church everywhere on earth, the Church of all times and all places, even Heaven, embracing all the saints who have persevered, and all the martyrs and confessors. Paul and Barnabas report their extraordinary and recent experience of God and of faith among the Gentiles before a council of the primitive church in Jerusalem, defending their faith and their Lord by citing the experience of Peter and the corroborative testimony of the Word of God in the Old Testament, which is then interpreted by the Apostle James. The leaders of the Church, with the consent of the whole gathering, give their dogmatic decision and a disciplinary command pertaining to the matter in question, which is to be transmitted to the Gentile Christian churches. The Evangelical exegete, E. Haenchen, speaks in this connection of a "public resolution which creates a valid canon law." The decisions which have been made are communicated to the mission churches and confirm them in the Catholic faith of the whole Church (Acts 15 and 16).[12]

[12] E. Haenchen, *Die Apostelgeschichte*, 1956, commenting on Acts 15:23,

Catholic Christian faith is therefore more than the individual, private, uncertain and uncontrolled experience and contemplation of God and of His revelation in Christ. Catholic faith finds its visible expression in established dogmatic definitions, disciplinary regulations and commands, and also in liturgical forms and traditions which are confirmed accordingly and can be made binding upon the whole Church everywhere. Consequently, we can speak of the Catholic faith in the words of the Athanasian Creed, for "except everyone do keep whole and undefiled" the dogmas of the Holy Trinity and the Incarnation of the Son of God, for example, "without doubt he shall perish everlastingly." The author of the Athanasian Creed was speaking no differently than the Apostle John who branded those who denied the Incarnation of the Son of God as false and evil spirits with whom the Church could have no association.

Johann Gerhard, in his reflections on the essence of the Catholic faith, notes that the Catholic consensus of the Church is based uniquely upon the "Catholic writings of the Prophets and Apostles." [13] Agreement with the canon of Holy Scripture is, of course, absolutely necessary, as the attitude of James at the council in Jerusalem clearly shows, in order that the "general harmony" (the Greek text calls it "symphony") of the Church's doctrinal decisions and definitions can be infallibly harmonized with revelation. In the long life of the Church, however, the necessary doctrinal definitions prove their divine legitimacy not merely because they seem to be in conformity with the written

---

points out that 16:4 shows that Luke considers the decree valid not only for those who are called "the brethren" in 15:23, but according to 15:19 it was meant for Gentile Christians generally (p. 398).

13 *Op. cit.*, p. 277.

Word in a formal or material way. For in the historical process there is within Scripture a development of the redeeming life and work of Christ. This development unfolds under the special conditions and necessities attendant on the people of God being led by the Holy Spirit through the "wilderness." All of this is recorded in Holy Scripture in a unique and binding manner, but the historical development reveals new concepts and new aspects of the blessings of revealed truth which are not explicitly set forth in Scripture. The dogmatic and disciplinary decision, for instance, which the Apostle James announced to the Gentile and Jewish Christian communities, which was then made binding upon them as the will and law of God, was a very arbitrary and restrictive decision expressed in terms that remind us of the Book of Leviticus. But the Holy Spirit had decided the matter through the Church's best qualified leaders in their general council,[14] and consequently it was a doctrinal definition which the Spirit of the Church made binding upon all. Or another example would be the Catholic decision of the Church that the Resurrection of the Lord be observed by the people of God as the holy day instead of the Jewish Sabbath. This is not found anywhere in the Old Testament Law, nor do the brief, occasional references in the New Testament to the Lord's Day contain any indication that the keeping of Sunday is henceforth to be considered as a sacred obligation of the Catholic religion. But every Catholic Christian keeps Sunday as by God's command and will. Transgression in this matter is regarded as seriously sinful. Similar examples of divine precepts which cannot be directly or explicitly derived from Holy Scripture would be

---

[14] Haenchen, *op. cit.*, p. 399, on Acts 15:28. "The heavenly and the legal, earthly instance are coexistent."

the regulation concerning infant baptism, the institutional form used in the sacrament of confession and in holy matrimony in the Church of our time.

The Catholic faith is therefore not to be read out of Holy Scripture in a merely literal and rational manner as Lutheran dogmatists have apparently thought. Nevertheless, the faith is certainly confirmed by Holy Scripture if we live and believe in communion with the Catholic Church. Anything in the Church's belief and practice that is not based on Scripture is consequently and demonstrably non-Catholic.

4. *The Church is called Catholic* as distinguished from all the sects which have separated from the universal Church because of their particular beliefs or religious practices and their un-Catholic separate existence. Sectarian schism generally implies doctrinal heresy also. An individual leader gathers together a band of followers among Catholic Christians who give their adherence to himself and his particular doctrine, laying great emphasis upon a particular part of the whole of Catholic faith and Scripture. This particular doctrine, isolated from Catholic scriptural evidence in its entirety and unduly stressed, is consequently an alteration of Catholic faith and destructive of Catholic unity. It is in this way that new sects originate which are named after their founders (Novatianists, Donatists, Arians) or after their special doctrines (Baptists, New-Apostolic Church, Adventists). The organization of sects of this kind in opposition to the Church "cannot be allowed by the Church which, as the visible and authentic communion of God's people, must include all of them uniformly and comprehensively." [15] Certainly the

[15] *Theologisches Wörterbuch zum Neuen Testament,* vol. 1, p. 182, article on Heresy.

Church must always emphasize the significance of being known as the *Catholic Church,* clearly distinguished from all the sects and "churches" which have "turned away from the general consensus of Catholic faith grounded in Holy Scripture, and have separated from the true Catholic Church" (Johann Gerhard).[16]

The appeal made by all heresies to particular biblical authors and their distinctive doctrines should not make the Catholic Church hesitant or uncertain. The Catholic Canon of Scripture, confirmed by decrees of the Catholic Church, contains a wide variety of different theological emphases which may occasionally seem to be logical contradictions of teachings of Christ concerning the grace of God, the responsibility of man, the nature of the Church and her organization. If we were merely to err slightly in our interpretation of the traditional teaching of Matthew or Luke or Paul, the whole Canon of Scripture would disintegrate, but the Spirit of the Church knows the intrinsic harmony of all the Scriptures and will safeguard them in order that the entire canon and consequently the Catholicity of the Church itself may be preserved and any partial or one-sided emphasis of biblical truth, or the possible loss of truth as a whole, may be prevented.

If our Church, with authentic Christian self-awareness, would designate itself as a "Catholic" Church, and not merely as Christian, we could avoid the suspicion of being regarded as a schismatical or heretical sect. The fundamental articles of the Hessian Church constitution still contain the following statement: "The Evangelical Church in Hesse and Nassau abides within the unity of the holy, universal and apostolic Church of Jesus Christ which is found wherever the pure word of God is preached and

16 *Op. cit.,* p. 277.

the sacraments are rightly and duly administered. This Church affirms that her faith is identical with the faith of the Ancient Church of the Creeds and one with the Fathers of the Augsburg Confession." Other Evangelical Churches not long ago decided to delete the word *Catholica* from the Creed and substituted "Christian" in its place. But this decision can only be considered as evidence of their further removal from the fundamental, historical and theological position of Reformed Christianity. The apparent Christian and "Evangelical" indifference toward all heresies and schisms is actually an eschatological sign. Paul and Peter both warned of the appearance of "pernicious sects" in the midst of God's people in the last days (I Cor. 1:10 ff; Acts 20:29; II Peter 2:1 ff). Jesus Himself, before His Ascension, instructed the Apostles regarding the heresies that would arise in the maturing life of the Church in the new dispensation. It matters little whether these sects are organized sociologically in the form of a small association or as a corporate body that is legally recognized as a "Church." They are not Catholic and that is decisive.

The preceding four aspects of the Catholicity of the Church have perhaps shown conclusively that Jesus Christ, since Pentecost, has been living and working within the historical, earthly form of His Body, the universal Church. We may quote from Ephesians 2:21, word for word. In Jesus Christ "the whole structure is closely fitted together and grows into a temple holy in the Lord." For Christ is the chief corner-stone through whom every particular Christian communion, with its own liturgy, theology and discipline, is built upon the foundation of the Apostles and Prophets in the visible structure of the one temple which God desires on earth: the one Catholic and Apos-

tolic Church. Catholicity is therefore not merely an ecclesiastical system, instituted and maintained by man,
which happens to be universal in scope. Christ Himself,
be it said plainly, is Catholic and universal. He has willed
and formed the one temple of God, and the whole of
Christendom should readily submit to His will and His
work. The Catholic Church in its total, historic and visible
form originated in this way and alone is identical with
the Church of the Apostles. The full heritage of apostolic
life, tradition and order will be found only in the totality
of all the Churches of Christ. Apostolicity "is not to be
newly derived from Holy Scripture in every generation
as if it were merely an idea with no history of its own."
It is inherent in the historic form of the Catholic Church
uniquely and exclusively.

The early Lutheran dogmatist was certainly mistaken
when, in defending his thesis against Bellarmine, he said,
"The Catholic name is not an intrinsic or essential characteristic (nota) of the Church." [17] On the contrary, whatever is Catholic necessarily belongs to the Christian and
Christ-like nature of the Church as the Body of Christ.
However, we must still make further inquiry into another
aspect of Catholicity which, plainly evident since the time
of Cyprian, Ambrose and Jerome, is considered problem-
atical by the Protestant mind; it is, of course, incontestable
that Catholicity is the historical form in which Christ is
building and preserving His Church.

5. *The Church is called Catholic* in so far as it abides
in union with the Church of Rome and with the Roman
Pontiff as its visible head. Whatever is Roman—or sanc-
tioned by the Bishop of Rome—is *ipso facto* Catholic. In
official ecclesiastical documents as far back as the thirteenth

17 *Op. cit.,* p. 393.

century, we read of the "most holy Roman Church, the mother and teacher of all the faithful." [18] In the words of Pope Pius IX, "There is no Catholic Church other than the Church which was founded on Peter, the one Rock." [19] *Roman* Catholic is the guarantee and realization and criterion of everything Catholic.

Contrary to the usual Protestant criticism of this definition of Catholicity, we shall neither disregard the hesitations concerning the practical use of the term "Catholic Church" in this sense, nor will we conceal our acknowledgement of the basic truth in the statement, "Catholic means Roman Catholic."

Since the schism of the Eastern Churches, and especially since the Reformation, the "most holy Roman Church" has acquired such importance in our conception of the Catholicity of the Church that it now seems necessary to use the adjective *Roman* as a distinguishing mark of the true Church. This term, by the way, was still readily used in the Augsburg Confession and the Apologia as an attribute of the Church in which we live and wish to live. It seems that *Roman* Catholic, like the words *holy* and *apostolic,* is a part of the Church's creed, as though it were an article of faith. The Roman character—*Romanitas*—of the Church has something of divine dignity about it. Christ, as the unifying cornerstone, cannot accomplish the building of the one Temple of God until whatever is *Roman,* i.e. Roman orthodoxy and the Roman conception of worship, together with the Roman pontiff's claim of

[18] Conc. Ludunense II, Denzinger No. 460. Innocent IV, in the year 1208, already declared "Corde credimus et ore confitemur unam Ecclesiam non haereticorum, sed sanctam Romanam, catholicam et apostolicam. . ." Denzinger No. 423. Also see Clement VI, 1351, Denzinger No. 570a.

[19] Denzinger No. 1686. See also Pius XII in *"De corpore mystico"* (1946) p. 59.

authority, becomes effective in determining and informing the vital faith of every particular Church and every individual Christian.

The word *Roman,* however, and the concept of *Romanitas,* have never been verbally expressed in the creed of the Church. The placing of *Roman* before the credal term *Catholic* would tend to compromise the Church's Catholic character, like our own adjective *Lutheran* which has a very un-Catholic connotation. The Church of Rome, moreover, is only one part of the great structure of the Temple of God. Like every particular Church, the Church of Rome has its own religious, theological, national, racial and historical limits. Can Catholicity, confined within these particular limits, still remain truly Catholic?

We know how many popes have been Italian, or Roman, in the past, and how difficult it has been for several centuries, and more especially in our own time, to gain or even compel acceptance of anything Catholic in the doctrinal, liturgical and canonical traditions of the particular Churches as contrasted with the prevailing doctrines, practices and decisions of Rome. The period of the Reformation, the early Middle Ages, and the nineteenth and twentieth centuries also, present many instances of this Roman predominance. It certainly does not seem to be attributable to the policies of individual popes or to special conditions of ecclesiastical life. There is apparently a prevailing tendency to make a theological principle of the subordination of everything Catholic to whatever is distinctively Roman, as to a spiritual, political, theological and canonical power which, like a kind of spiritual straight-jacket, tightly envelops the whole Catholic world. This "Romanism" and Roman centralism became intolerable to the kings and nations of the late Middle Ages, and

were unbearable to the Reformers, politically, canonically
and financially (the Sale of Indulgences!). Meanwhile, it
seems to us that a canonical and theological Romanism
has been set forth in pronounced and rigid form in the
Codex juris canonici. Roman theology, Roman opinions,
Roman authorities, always take precedence whenever it
is a question of making disciplinary or canonical decisions
and also those of a liturgical or theological kind. Consequently, it seems that the unity and growth of the "Catholic" Temple of God becomes increasingly more like the
administration of a purely human technical system—
the Roman Catholic system in this instance—than like
the unity of the particular, integral parts within the one
Temple through Jesus Christ, the corner-stone. We have
in mind especially the distinctive liturgical, canonical and
doctrinal techniques of Rome, gradually developed, and
used for the purpose of extending and maintaining the
"Catholic" Church, but which really *prevent* the full
growth of the one Body *in Christo*. Were it not for this
Roman technique, the tragedy of the Reformation would
never have been carried to such extremes. Those who are
familiar with the best authors of ecclesiastical history will
readily agree with this statement. We must therefore still
consider the *protest* of the Reformers made in behalf of
the real Catholicity of the Church against excessive Romanism as authentically Christian and genuinely Catholic.
Nevertheless, we must also acknowledge the unquestionable aspect of truth in the earlier and authentic meaning
of the terms *Roman* and *Catholic*. Catholicism is understandable only in its complete, historical dimension, for
since man's entering into communion with God through
the incarnation of the Son, and the resurrection and ascension of the crucified Savior, the "whole Christ" *(as*

Head and Body) exists uniquely in concrete, human form.
This means the temporal and historical existence of an
historically recognizable people, earthly and temporal, and
yet in close union with God, because they are the very incarnation and fulfillment of His eternal purposes. We can
agree with Yves Congar, "The Christian meaning of Time,
as the era of the Church, lies in the cooperation or col-
laboration of man as a positive contribution toward the
ultimate end: the Kingdom of God (or, meaning the same
thing, the 'Temple'). The Christian mystery is the formation of the Second Adam within the nature of the first, the
entrance of time into eternity based upon the descent of
eternity into time. It is within the Church that Christ
exists in the world and finds His fulfillment in its very
substance" (*Der Laie,* 1957, p. 116).

Certain dangers and weaknesses of Roman Catholicism
may be attributable to the "ostensible needs of mankind"
and to the general tendency toward concreteness, but this
does not provide any clue to the real, theological understanding of Roman Catholicity as Hans Grünewald recently supposed in his book (*Römische und pneumatische
Katholizität,* 1956, p. 33 ff). Grünewald himself suggested
that we would have to delve profoundly into the Lutheran
theology of the "nature of spirit" which endures *"in-alio-
esse"* as in nonexistence (*op. cit.,* p. 33 ff). For it is the
spirit of Christ Himself, the incarnate Lord, and not
merely a decadent Christendom, which is impelling us
toward concreteness in the historical forms, places and
times of the Body of Christ. The visible Temple of God
which Christ is building upon the foundation of all the
apostolic Churches on earth has therefore, and necessarily,
a fixed spatial and temporal starting-point and rallying-
point. An earthly people, composed of men of all nations,

comprising the People of God, requires a continuing and visible center of unity. Israel maintained the royal city of Jerusalem, chosen and sanctified by Almighty God as the focal point for the gathering of the Twelve Tribes. It was an especially painful moment when Jesus had to inform His people that this same Jerusalem would soon cease to be the vital center of the People of God. However, immediately after Pentecost, the primitive church of Jerusalem temporarily became the center of the emergent People of the New Covenant, and to this church was committed the care of the most important concerns and needs of the Apostles and all the mission churches everywhere.[20]

After the catastrophe of the year 70 A.D., another center —Rome—came into view. It was the very center of the world in those days, sanctified by the deeds and deaths of the apostles Peter and Paul. In the light of sacred history, and particularly in Luke's Gospel and the Acts of the Apostles, the mention of the "storming" of Rome through the missionary preaching of Paul is a direct reference to the future course of the divine formation of the Church. Rome, the heart of the world, now becomes the center of

20 "It honored the Church of Antioch and also emphasized the authority of Jerusalem when they let the decree of the Church of Jerusalem be carried by a special delegation." Haenchen, *op. cit.*, p. 397, on Acts 15. On "The authority of Jerusalem" also see p. 406 and p. 408, "Missions to various cities and countries were subject to Jerusalem in one way or another . . . Jerusalem was the spiritual head of the *corpus christianum* and certainly as the *sedes apostolica* where the eye-witnesses of the earthly life and the resurrection of the Lord were living."

Ethelbert Stauffer, in his essay, *Die Urkirche,* in Historia Mundi, volume IV, *Römisches Weltreich und Christentum,* p. 307 f., states conclusively, "Six years after the death of the Roman apostles Jerusalem was destroyed. Now the church located in the world's capital entered into possession of the heritage of Jerusalem's ecclesiastical leadership. . . . Rome will soon surpass both Antioch and Ephesus and become the New Jerusalem, the city which the Lord has chosen (Deut. 17:10), the Holy City of Christendom."

the new People of the Covenant, an earthly representation of the heavenly Jerusalem which came down upon earth with the Messias, and Paul speaks of the Christian community in Rome in glowing terms, "because your faith is proclaimed all over the world" (Rom. 1:8). The Church of Rome, sanctified by the blood of the Apostles, becomes therefore a representative, eschatological prototype of the whole of God's world as it is and will become. The Church of Rome, by the will of God Himself, becomes the symbol of the all-inclusive Catholic Church.

Ancient documents which have come down to us indicate that the Church of Rome was very early accorded a special role in the superstructure of the universal Church. In the year 96 A.D., the author of the first Epistle of Clement,[21] as the spokesman of the whole People of God "who live like Roman subjects," admonishes the Church of Corinth in serious, authoritative and brotherly tones to correct the internal abuses of their ecclesiastical community. He censures, exhorts, cautions, entreats, and expresses the hope that the Roman messengers "may the more quickly report the peace and concord which is prayed for and earnestly desired by us that we also may the more speedily rejoice over your good order." Various Evangelical scholars have commented upon the concept of the Church which we find in this first Epistle of Clement. In the *Lehrbuch der Dogmengeschichte,* I, p. 444, Harnack declares, "This letter to the Corinthians proves that already by the end of the first century the Roman Church knew the best terms to use in the simultaneous expression of allegiance, love and authority." Erich Caspar, in his history of the papacy (*Geschichte des Papstums,* I, 1939, p. 5), states, "Unmistakably, the ecclesiastical concept so prom-

---

21 *Die Apostolischen Väter,* ed. Bihlmeyer, p. 35 and p. 70.

inently emphasized in the first Epistle of Clement was very similar to that which prevailed in the primitive church of Jerusalem. In Rome, authority and tradition as essential characteristics of the Church are only mentioned briefly in passing. . . . It is not a question of a deviation from the original position after the charismata had diminished, but was a renewal of something which had existed from the beginning. . . . For the saying about the 'pillars' of the primitive church in Jerusalem (Gal. 2:9) was adopted by the Epistle of Clement in which Peter and Paul are called the 'greatest and most upright pillars.' Rome had now become what Jerusalem once had been. God, Christ, the Apostles, the first converts, are a concatenation cited in the Roman epistle of Clement, which is continued in Rome itself" (p. 10-14). Ethelbert Stauffer calls the first Epistle of Clement "the most informative document" regarding the supersession of Jerusalem by *Ecclesia Romana*. Stauffer notes that the use of the expression *send back* in the statement: "Send back speedily unto us our messengers" (I Clem. 65,1), is not merely a special kind of biblical phrase but also a form of Roman imperial command. The Roman judge in a province of the empire *sent back* a messenger or a packet of documents to the imperial capital or to the court of the emperor (Acts 25:21). Clement of Rome doubtless also knew this administrative terminology of the imperial government and used it effectively." A few years later, Bishop Ignatius of Antioch writes to the Christian community at Rome, addressing it emphatically as the Church "which presides in the country of the Romans, worthy of divine esteem, and of glory and praise and honor, worthy of victory, deserving sanctification, and pre-eminent in charity, keeping the Law of Christ. . . . You have never envied anyone;

you have taught others." [22] Adolph von Harnack (op. cit., 445) remarks on Ignatius (Ad Romanos, Proem., 3, 1 and 4, 3), "It is clearly apparent that Ignatius acknowledged the primacy of the Roman Church among the sister-churches, and that the zealous activity of this Church in assisting and instructing other Churches was well known to himself." In the fourth edition, page 488, Harnack makes still another interesting observation: "The expression, Head of the Brotherhood of Love, is used by Ignatius in his letter to the faithful of Magnesia in order to indicate the dignity of the Bishop and the priests, respectively, in relation to the ecclesiastical community." Seventy years later, Bishop Irenaeus of Lyons, in his treatise against the doctrines of the false gnostics, wrote, "With this Church, because of its superior pre-eminence, every Church must agree, that is the faithful of all countries, for in communion with this Church the apostolic tradition has always been preserved by the faithful everywhere." [23] In

[22] Op. cit., p. 97, 1 ff. and p. 98, 6.

[23] Regarding the disputed translation of the passage on "Unmasking and Refutation of the false gnosis" (not in the original Greek text but found in the Latin version), and especially of the words "potentior principalitas" and "convenire" see F. X. Seppelt, "Geschichte der Päpste," Vol. 1, 1954, p. 26 f.

Father Nautin O.S.B., has published an admirable criticism of the use of this text of Irenaeus in behalf of the Roman primacy. (Irenaeus, Adv. haer. III, 3,2.; "Church of Rome or Universal Church?" in Revue de l'histoire des religions, 101 (1957), pp. 37-78. Compare this with the statement of B. Botte O.S.B., "A propos de l'Adv. haer. III, 3,2, de St. Irène," in Irenikon, published by the Benedictine Abbey of Amay, Chevetogne, Belgium, Vol. XXX, 2nd Quarter, 1957, pp. 156-163.) "Ad hanc enim ecclesiam. . . . necesse est omnem convenire ecclesiam"—Nautin contends—has reference to the whole Church which possesses true bishops of the apostolical succession, as for instance, Rome. Irenaeus had previously mentioned Churches whose bishops were of this succession and he then speaks of Rome by name as the type of the true Church whose episcopate stands in the apostolical descent and tradition. "The potentior principalitas is not the superiority of the Church of Rome over the other Churches, but is rather the superiority of the Universal Church over the sects" another passage, Harnack continues, "Irenaeus expressly accords the highest rank to the Church of Rome among those churches which had been founded by the Apostles because her voice was the most esteemed and most impressive in all Christendom. This *principalitas*, i.e. authenticity in relation to other churches, was vested in all of the apostolic churches, but a *potentior principalitas* was acknowledged in the Church of Rome in so far as it excelled all the other churches as *ecclesia maxima et omnibus cognita*. The Roman Community was esteemed in those days as the true *conservatrix traditionis*" (*op. cit.*, p. 445 and footnote 3, p. 446, or in the Fourth Edition I, p. 488). It was not the conceit and pride of the Christians of Rome, but "the supreme power of the Almighty Father and of Jesus Christ" (Ignatius [24]) which singled out the Church of Rome as the model, the mother and teacher of all the faithful, like Jerusalem when her final renewal as the Mother of all the children of God was proclaimed by the Prophet (Isaias 66:10 ff). Tertullian (160-240 A.D.), referring to Valentinus, the gnostic who had fallen away from the Church into heresy, expressed the opinion, "He has separated from that Church which possesses the authenticity of the rule of faith" (*Adv. Valentinos*, c. 3). This emphasis upon the authenticity of a rule of faith through the Church of Rome was underlined by Harnack in a significant comment concerning the history of the canon: "The New Testament canon with the Apostolic-Catholic

(Botte, *op. cit.*, p. 158). Nautin's attempt is praiseworthy, but it contains linguistic difficulties. Are we really not to assume that the expression "ad hanc enim ecclesiam" refers to the Church of Rome? But even if Rome were regarded as merely the type of a Church possessing true apostolical succession, it still remains a remarkable fact that Irenaeus named Rome as the principal example.

[24] *Op. cit.*, p. 96, 17.

predicates and with its exclusiveness is primarily traceable
to the Church of Rome. It has now been proved that the
whole series of New Testament books in their canonical
and universally accepted versions were derived from Rome.
Finally, new evidence of the greatest value indicates that
from the third century the versions of the West, i.e. the
Roman texts of the New Testament, entered into the
texts of the Oriental biblical manuscripts. These data
clearly prove that the Eastern Churches corrected their
own versions by comparison with the New Testament received from Rome in those days. It was with special reference to Rome that an authentic list of Bishops extending
back to the Apostles was prepared" (*op. cit.*, p. 443 ff).

This pre-eminence of the Church of Rome was also
based upon the special position and dignity of her *bishops,*
widely acknowledged from the middle of the third century
when the primacy of Rome was explicitly attributed to the
Roman pontiff's legitimate succession to the Chair of Peter.
Pope Stephen I refused to sanction the re-baptism of heretics expressly because he was the occupant of Peter's
throne.[25] His contemporary episcopal colleague, Cyprian,

---

[25] Seppelt, (*op. cit.*, p. 52). Today it is hardly a tenable thesis that the
primacy of Peter in relation to the other Apostles, and even in regard to
Paul, cannot be found in the documents of the New Testament. Karl
Ludwig Schmidt, in *Theologischen Wörterbuch zum Neuen Testament,*
Vol. III (1938), p. 226, plainly declares: "Peter also played a much greater
role in the forming of opinion through Paul than is admitted in the controversy between Protestantism and Catholicism. . . . Peter was chosen
for a special purpose, and although he became stubborn and obdurate, he
remained specially chosen because he was the *fundamentum ecclesiae.*"
However, as early as 1902, Carl Weizsäcker, in *Das Apostolische Zeitalter
der christlichen Kirche,* 3rd ed., p. 12, stated, "Peter is unquestionably the
leader of the primitive Church. When Paul was converted to the Christian
religion he had made his decision in his own mind and in the Holy Spirit
who had called him, but when this decision was finally made, he resolved
immediately to get in touch with the Christian community, as anyone else
would have done. However, this did not mean personal contact with the

may not have acknowledged the Roman pontiff's primacy of jurisdiction as we know it today, but it is obvious from Cyprian's writings that he also revered the Church of Rome as "the See of Peter and the principal Church from which the unity of the priesthood had its rise." [26] Even earlier, toward the end of the second century, Bishop Irenaeus, in his criticism of the harsh decision of Pope Victor in the controversy concerning the date of Easter did not attack the Pope's right to excommunicate particular Churches from the communion of the universal Church. This attitude of Irenaeus clearly proves that the position of the Church of Rome as the representative and spiritual center of Catholic Christendom was evidently associated with the idea of the Roman pontiff as the vicar of all the Churches of Christ and as the successor of St. Peter. In regard to Victor's procedure in the Easter controversy, Harnack remarks (*op. cit.*, p. 448), "How did Victor dare to issue such an edict if it were not well-established and generally recognized that doctrinal disputes should be settled by the Roman Church? . . . or if he were not regarded, in a special sense, as the guardian of the deposit of faith?" Similarly,

---

whole community which would have been impossible by this time, for obvious reasons. But Paul set out to find Peter, and this was sufficient. It was only for this purpose and with this hope clearly in mind that he went to Jerusalem to become acquainted with this man. In him Paul saw the whole of Christendom down to the present day. Peter was singled out for leadership by the Master Himself."

See also E. Stauffer's historical and theological comments on the problem of Peter in *Theologie des Neuen Testaments,* p. 15 ff, and in his essay, *"Geschichte Jesu"* in Historia Mundi, *op. cit.,* p. 187. Jesus recognizes Peter as the responsible leader of the infant Church. Without the protophany of Peter, and without the definite call of the Risen Lord, the special position of Peter in the primitive Church would be historically quite unintelligible. For Peter was not a man to create such a special position through the "strength of his personality."

26 Seppelt, *op. cit.,* p. 56, quotes Cyprian: "Petri cathedra atque ecclesia principalis, unde unitas sacerdotalis exorta est."

Hans Lietzmann, in his history of the ancient church points out, "For the first time the unity of the Catholic Church was displayed in a number of synodal decisions, and the unanimous opinion was in harmony with what the Roman Church had defined as orthodox. It was unquestionable that Rome had incited and dominated the whole controversy and that the Roman position was proved to be right" (*Geschichte der alten Kirche,* Vol. II, 2nd edition, 1953, p. 247).

The development and growth of the holy Catholic Church, accomplished in accordance with the manifest purpose of Christ's will and spirit, is inseparably connected with the primacy of the Roman Church and of her bishop. It is a simple matter of fact that from the end of the first century the Church of Rome, together with her bishop, has had an immeasurable part in the expansion of the Catholic Church throughout the world. This fact is not weakened because Leo the Great was the first to quote the passage in Matthew 16:18 to bring the claim of universal primacy to the theological awareness of the Church. Particular incidents, and the decisions of various popes (Victor, Stephen, Dionysius, Julius I, Damasus, Siricius, Innocent I) together with the proceedings of the Nicene Council and the synod of Sardica clearly reveal the more or less excellent efforts of the Roman pontiffs in exercising leadership among all the bishops and patriarchs, like Peter among the twelve apostles. Erich Caspar's study of the early succession of Roman pontiffs in *Die älteste römische Bischofsliste* (2, p. 472), says, "The Catholic idea of the Church, already prevalent in the primitive Christian community of Jerusalem, was based upon authority and apostolic tradition, and was also very ancient in Rome. The proven line of Roman succession indicates the authenticity of this tradition. However, the idea of an apostolical succession, definitely associated with certain names, conjoined with this same idea of the Church, is also very ancient and constitutes the spiritual basis and strength of episcopacy." E. Stauffer, in *Die Theologie des Neuen Testaments* (Fourth Edition, p. 15), reaches similar conclusions in his commentary on Peter and the early Church: "The Church idea (like the concepts of primacy and succession), is no early papal device but is even older than Christendom itself. This fact is increasingly acknowledged today." Even Günther Bornkamm, the Protestant authority on the New Testament, had to admit that the passage in Matthew 16:18 "already established the Church as an institution endowed with full teaching and governing authority, and identified with the monarchical episcopate of a certain apostle now has its clearly defined status between the Resurrection and the Last Judgment" (*Jesus von Nazareth*, 1957, p. 171, f). Bornkamm, however, does not consider this passage in Matthew as a true saying of Jesus but rather as a special tradition of a small minority of the early Church who put this saying into the mouth of Jesus. Nevertheless, we cannot deny that in the process of the life and growth of the Catholic Church since Pentecost the Church of Rome, with her bishop as the successor of St. Peter in the primatial See, has acquired a divine dignity and a special role in the economy of salvation as the servant of Christ, the chief corner-stone. The Church is Catholic because, in a special manner, it is associated with the Church of Rome and with her bishop. Orthodoxy in faith, and the authority of the priesthood and the episcopate acting in Christ's stead, are by divine precept ob-

tained and preserved only through the new Christ-Life of
the Church in her historical form. The See of Rome and
the authority of its bishop are closely identified with this
particular, historical form. Ethelbert Stauffer considers
Clement's pastoral epistle of 96 A.D. as the beginning of
the history of the universal Church of Rome. "It begins
with the *interpretatio Romana* of the Jewish and early
Christian canon law. The Roman emperor had destroyed
Jerusalem . . . Now, however, the Roman pontiff executes
the ecclesiastico-political will and testament of Jerusalem.
Roma aeterna caput ecclesiae. Four centuries later the
Roman pontiff is the heir and testamentary executor of
the Caesars. *Roma aeterna caput orbis Christiani" (Die
Urkirche, op. cit.,* p. 308).

We Lutherans certainly have our own experiences as
evidence that God can also "act otherwise." But what God
can and will do in special circumstances does not dispense
us from His revealed will and His explicit commands.
The Holy Trinity is certainly not bound absolutely by
any ecclesiastical forms in regard to the economy of salvation, but the Church cannot emancipate herself from
them without destroying the divine economy in the world.

A Protestantism which is no longer aware of the spiritual coherence of the incarnation, the ascension, the history
of the Church (as the living Body of Christ), and of the
Church's liturgy, the administration of the sacraments and
the development of doctrine, together with priestly authority and the faith of the Church, will certainly remain
blind to such insights. But this is all the more reason for
us to give serious thought to the remarks of the Lutheran
general superintendent and theologian, A. F. C. Vilmar,
who wrote an article on the papacy in the nineteenth cen-

tury.[27] He made no attempt to conceal the Evangelical criticism of the "monarchical" concept of the papacy, but he claimed that the two African bishops, Cyprian and Optatus, rightly emphasized "that the unity of the Western Churches is dependent upon the episcopal See of Rome as the Chair of Peter. This, of course, is understandable because of the maternal role which the Roman Church assumed in its relations with the other Churches of the West. Additionally, however, in deciding controversial issues, this episcopal See which had been under the special care of the Apostles and especially the most noble Apostles for a longer time and was recognized as the principal See by all parties and factions, had to uphold the living tradition of Christian faith and order in their orthodox integrity, and therefore both naturally and inevitably it became the spiritual center for all the Churches that were dependent upon it. The primacy of the See of Rome was also established through firm and steadfast fidelity to the living apostolic tradition, and this was in sharp contrast with the inconstancy of the Orientals during the Arian controversies of the fourth century. Consequently, the primacy of the Bishop of Rome among the other Patriarchs in the Eastern Churches was self-evident to everyone. Nevertheless, all of this shows that the privileged position of the Roman pontiff was the result of the historical and natural development of the Christian Church, or even more truly the result of the guidance of the Holy Spirit, and that it was by a gradual process that the primacy was developed into the supremacy and importance which the Roman pontiff has claimed since the end of

27 "The Papacy," an article written for the *Staats-und Gesellschaftslexikon* by H. Wagner (Berlin, 1859-1866), reprinted in *Theo. Kirchl. Aufsätze*, ed. K. Ramge, 1938, p. 113 f.

the fourth century. . . . The importance of the papacy to
the universal Christian Church is based upon two central
facts: first of all it is through the papacy that the unity of
the Church is symbolized, as Cyprian correctly pointed out
long ago. Secondly, it was through the papacy that the in-
violable rule was proclaimed and made effective that the
Church should only be governed by itself as a spiritual
authority and not by any secular power or by the totality
of the Church's members. The complete loss of the papacy,
if such a thing were possible, and this is simply inconceivable, would result in the disintegration of all the particular Churches into small and ever smaller groups, the
very atomizing of the Church, and the overwhelming predominance of crude unbelief, absolute anarchy and finally
the total ruin of Christianity."

The usual Protestant claim that our divided Christendom will be healed, not by a return to Rome but rather
by conversion to Jesus Christ, is actually, when formulated
in such a way, an alternative that is theologically false.
However, our *critical* question must nevertheless by given
a hearing: Should Romanism and papal centralism (a human and earthly, legalistic and monarchical "transformation") so dominate the See of Rome and its bishop that
the very spirit of Christ is alienated and "Rome" becomes
a hindrance to the preservation and fulfillment of the
whole Catholic body, with the unfortunate consequence
that non-Roman churches and bishops (not merely since
the political and ecclesiastical rivalry of Constantinople
and Rome!) should become even more interested in Matthew 20:25-26 than in verses 27 and 28? Certainly Cyprian's complaints to the Council of Carthage (256 A.D.)
against the "haughtiness" of Bishop Stephen of Rome, who
"uses tyrannical fear in order to compel his colleagues to

submit to himself," [28] were evidently not based on thin air. No doubt Stephen's decision concerning the validity of heretical baptism was Catholic and Christian, while Cyprian's opinion, and that of his eighty-seven fellow-bishops was not. But Stephen's procedure (obviously very legalistic and monarchical) in appealing to the Roman tradition without giving any hearing at all to the opposite arguments, while demanding everyone's submission to himself as the successor of St. Peter, under threat of excommunication, was certainly deficient in that genuine spiritual outlook and guidance which alone can hold the Church together in unity. Intercommunion between Rome and the African Churches, as well as the Bishops of Asia Minor, was suspended for a while because of this. The breach between Rome and the Eastern Churches (1054 A.D.) can also be attributed to the increasing presumption and infringing self-assertion of the See of Rome, even though many other factors were important in this estrangement. We find very little of the humility of the Washing of the Feet but a great deal of political passion and inordinate desire for power which were concealed behind the most exalted ecclesiastical titles. The critical protest of the Reformation was aimed at the danger of Roman and papal legalism to the Catholicity of the Church.

The most severe criticism of the theological theory and the actual functioning of the Roman papacy in the Church neither can nor may contradict the historical judgment that in the Church of Rome and in her bishop, uniting and governing all the Churches and Bishops, the Catholic and Apostolic Church has found an abiding center of the highest pastoral and teaching office, established by the

28 Seppelt, *op. cit.*, p. 53.

Holy Spirit and by Christ's own institution. Bishop Grosseteste (1175-1253 A.D.), bishop of Lincoln, for example,
openly opposed Pope Innocent IV to his face when the
pope was residing in Lyons. He publicly accused him of
responsibility for the guilt of the papacy of his time in its
spiritual neglect of Christendom. "God forbid that this
See will ever be the cause of apostasy and open schism in
the future." The pope, to whom Christ gave full authority
"for building but not for destroying" stood in danger of
sharing the "pernicious throne" on which Lucifer and the
Antichrist are seated.[29] A Catholic bishop thus allowed
himself to make these and other reproaches against the
pope, but it never occurred to him that he should leave
the Roman Catholic Church or separate himself from the
communion of its Chief Bishop as a matter of principle.
Even if the Roman pontiff has occasionally acted as the
"Antichrist" openly "advocating godless doctrine and false
worship" (as Luther and Melanchthon declared), would
it not be exactly for this reason that we would conclude
that Rome and the See of the Roman pontiff really *is* the
Holy See of the Catholic and Apostolic Church? According
to the preaching of the prophets and the apostles the "adversary" is to be enthroned upon the Holy Place (Mt.
24:15) "in the Temple of God" (II Thess. 2:4; Daniel
11:36). However, the "holy Temple" of God, since Pentecost, is "the true dwelling of the living Rock," the holy
Catholic and Apostolic Church (Eph. 2:21; I Pet. 2:5).
Where the Antichrist establishes his throne we shall surely
find the new "heavenly Jerusalem" (Heb. 12:22), the city
of the living God, just as Antiochus and the soldiers of

29 On Grosseteste's discussion with Innocent IV, see: *Realenzyklopädie
für protestantische Theologie und Kirche,* 3rd ed., Vol. 7, p. 193 ff; Ferdi-
nand Piper, Evang. Kalender, Vol. 19-21, 1868, p. 127 ff.

Titus, with human hands, perpetrated the "abomination of desolation" upon the divine city of Jerusalem.

II

All of these definitions of the Catholicity of the Church, as we have presented them in this chapter, were originally acknowledged by the Reformers and the authors of the Augsburg Confession. A Church that would be wholly independent of Rome was never in Luther's program at any time. The Augsburg Confession affirms that its doctrinal declarations contain nothing which "deviates from the Bible or from the Catholic Church, or from the Roman Church. . . . Therefore, they judge harshly who insist that we be regarded as heretics." [30] They appealed to the ancient ecumenical councils, and to the Fathers of the Church and to the saints. They considered the Catholic condemnations of anti-Catholic sects and heresies as their very own. They waited, as "Augsburg brethren in the faith" for a universal council under the presidency of Rome, in which the objectionable abuses and conditions would be corrected and theological questions would be fully discussed. In the year 1532, Luther wrote to the Duke of Prussia, warning him to guard against strange and fanciful notions of the Lord's Supper; "It is dangerous and dreadful to hear or believe anything contrary to the unanimous witness, faith and doctrine of the entire holy, Christian Church, universally held throughout the world for over fifteen hundred years from the beginning until the present day. . . . I would prefer that the philosophy and law, not only of factious spirits but of all emperors, kings and princes also, should bear witness against me,

30 Bekenntnisschriften, *op. cit.*, p. 82.

than hear or see one jot or tittle of the holy Christian Church opposed to me. The articles of faith which have been held unanimously by all of Christendom from the beginning until now are not to be taken lightly." [31]

Even those professing specifically "Evangelical" doctrines of justification through grace alone for the sake of Christ, and of the universal priesthood, the all-sufficiency of the once offered sacrifice of Christ, and the distinction between law and gospel, were making efforts to prove that these doctrines were derived from the Catholic Church's own heritage of faith. "Evangelical" truth is also Catholic truth, and consequently the Catholic Church must give "Evangelical" emphases and insights adequate expression if it is not to become a sectarian, heretical church.

The aim of the Reformers to lead the Church to a purer form of Catholicity has miscarried. For centuries we have been seeking the reason for this failure only in the reactions of those who oppose the Reformers, and there is doubtless a great deal to be said about this. But it must now be admitted that the Reformers failed to present "Evangelical" truth in such a way that it could still be recognized as relevant to *Catholic* truth. With the passing of time Evangelical doctrinal statements became more and more of a threat to Catholic teaching and were gradually losing their Catholic content. The Evangelical doctrine of the universal priesthood is presented in an un-Catholic manner if it excludes the idea of the special priesthood. The Catholic Church has never been without specially ordained priests at any time. The Evangelical doctrine of the all-sufficiency of the sacrifice of Calvary is expressed in an un-Catholic sense if it omits the presence and oblation of the sacrifice of Christ and the sacrifice of

31 Weimarer Ausgabe Vol. 30, 3; p. 552 f.

the Church in divine worship and Christian life. Sacrifice has always been of central importance in the Catholic Church. The Evangelical doctrine of the inspiration of the individual by the Holy Spirit is un-Catholic if it means that we can dispense with the episcopal teaching office of the Church. The Catholic Church has never been without the apostolic authority of her bishops. Many additional examples could be cited.

Champions of the Evangelical cause—contrary to the original aims of the Reformation—have supposed that their Catholicity could only be proved by an open breach with Rome and with the Pope. However, in the circumstances this breach was not only inevitable but was even required by Christian faith in this instance, and in fact it was necessary for *both* sides, for each side was right and wrong in its own way.

But the Evangelical group lost their concrete Catholic connection and status because of this schism, and they lost indispensable Catholic means of grace: the ecumenical episcopate, the Catholic liturgy, the office of the priesthood, the tradition of canon law and of a common Christian order, the advantages of an authoritative pastoral and teaching office. Moreover, continuing in their sectarian existence from century to century as national or local churches, they lost still more of that Catholic heritage of grace which had originally been taken with them into their "Evangelical" schism. This separation from the main body of Christ's Church in its totality resulted in the gradual loss of the remaining Catholic heritage which they earnestly intended to conserve. In the Evangelical Churches of our day this Catholic heritage from the Reformation Era has been reduced to a bare minimum, and the question arises whether anything derived originally from the

Catholic Church will much longer be found in them. We shall have to give serious thought to a consideration of whether, through theological programs or pious wishes, we can still recover even a part of the Catholic heritage which the post-Reformation generation, although no longer in communion with the Western Church, still possessed, especially after our deliberate and continuing refusal of communion with this Church for nearly five centuries. In any case, all efforts in this direction meet with great theological and practical difficulties. Spiritual treasures and ordinances of the Body of Christ cannot be restored outside the Catholic communion of the Church through any act of faith, however sincere, and certainly not by means of any ecclesiastical legislation. Furthermore, this kind of thinking is unspiritual and un-Catholic in regard to the Church. Apostolicity is not a theory to be read about in the Bible and then realized in practice. It is the vital, heavenly and spiritual grace found in the preaching of the Gospel, and in the sacraments, the canon law, the ordinances and liturgy of the Catholic Church on earth. Either we share in this spiritual treasury through membership in the Church or we separate from it, and wither away with the passing of time.

The reasons for this decline of Catholic life among us are to be sought in the theological and religious conditions of the late Middle Ages. This must be said in our own defense because of the continuing Roman attempt to place all the blame on the personal character and life of Martin Luther. It is the Catholic Church as a whole, and not merely the Protestant or Roman party, or the pope, that failed to complete the Reformation that was called forth by the Spirit and Word of God. In this respect, each party has made its own negative contribution.

From the beginning the Evangelical demand for reform contained a hidden notion of the Church which was un-Catholic and alien. But this had originated in the Catholic climate of the Middle Ages. Antagonism between the philosophical schools of Nominalism and Realism (i.e. Universalism) since the fourteenth century, the emancipation of theological scholarship from ecclesiastical authority in order to facilitate the pursuit of undistorted truth by a direct return to the original sources of Holy Scripture (Humanism), the wide divergence between theological and popular conceptions of the liturgy, the late medieval Gothic and mystical subjectivism which was already well under way, as well as the exaltation of the individual over the communal and universal, as required by Nominalism, were intellectual tendencies and philosophical methods of the Catholic Middle Ages which made their particular contribution to the way in which the Evangelical demand for Reformation was conceived and carried out. They caused the Evangelical-Catholic purposes of the Holy Spirit to be expressed in ways that were bound to endanger the very structure of the Church if they did not destroy it completely. Various political and social factors were of considerable importance also.

On the Roman side the reaction was almost exclusively defensive. Many of the hierarchy, and even simple secular priests and layfolk, refused to make the response of reflection and conversion which the Evangelical demand had called for. Prelates and theologians were so shocked by the offensive, strangely un-Catholic connotations of the Evangelical demands that they were only concerned about defending the Church against anything that was un-Catholic. Only a very few, isolated theologians made any effort to really understand the Catholic and Christian content of Evangelical aims and objectives, and to classify them within the whole of Catholic thought conformably with the philosophical and theological concepts of the Scholasticism of their time. Although this was beyond their capacity, they were however more capable in this endeavor than their opponents!

The reluctance of Roman and Italian theologians of the Curia to participate in serious discussion of Luther's "Germanic" theology of conscience and experience, which had originated in a wholly different environment than their own theology (we need only mention the great Lutheran themes of temptation, faith, and assurance of salvation), so greatly impeded the Council of Trent concerning the reform of the Church that a new impetus was given to the profound evangelical purposes of the Lutheran Reformation.

The Reformers finally found it necessary to respond to the defensive reaction of the western hierarchy with an equally emphatic repudiation of Roman leadership over Christendom. In such circumstances, of course, a Christian and Catholic decision of conscience cannot be condemned, but in this instance it resulted in the loss of Catholicity in the newly-formed "Catholic" separatist Church that was surnamed *Lutheran*. Johann Gerhard, the orthodox Lutheran dogmatist of the seventeenth century, quoted long liturgical prayers of Ambrose, Basil, Chrysostom, Damascene and Thomas Aquinas in his writings on the Lord's Supper, and concluded with St. Thomas' hymn, *Adoro te devote latens deitas,* and the hymn of the Church, *O panis dulcissime.*[32] But his discussions with the "papal" theologian, Bellarmine, unfortunately indicate how far this Catholic-minded Lutheran soon became estranged from

[32] *Loco citato,* locus 21, p. 251 ff.

the Catholic arguments of the "papists" and from Holy Scripture itself.

When we consider the situation inversely, we see how little appreciation was shown to the papal theologian for having included the hopes and interests of Protestants, sympathetically, in his defense of the Catholic cause. The separation of Evangelical Christians from the Catholic Church, however unavoidable it may have seemed to responsible men of that era, unquestionably diminished the Catholicity of the Roman Church. Rome needed the separated Evangelical part as greatly as the latter needed Rome in order that the one Church might show forth her Catholicity to the whole world. This point of view seems to be diametrically opposed to the thought and outlook of the sixteenth century. In those days, both the Reformed Christians and the Roman Catholic Church were hurling anathemas against each other. Each section of Christendom has been convinced ever since that only in separation from the other can it constitute the true, Catholic Church. These historical decisions are admittedly irreformable, but for that very reason they are not conclusive. In the course of four hundred years they have produced entirely new historical developments—theological, religious, political and cultural. The same adversaries are still ranged against each other, but it is no longer the same accusation of the sixteenth century that we make against each other today. The divine mandate has changed, and a wholly new call of God to conversion is now perceptible in the mysterious interweaving of guilt and truth. For us Lutherans it means a call to Catholic fulfillment. This implies a Catholic fulfillment of both the *form* and the *doctrines* of Evangelical Christianity, but also of our Evangelical mission to the Roman Catholic mother church.

Our Evangelical witness regarding the justification of the sinner, and our conceptions of the Church, the Mass, confession, law and gospel, jurisdiction and authority, require a solid basis in the Catholic totality of Scripture and the Church, if they are ever to possess universal Christian validity. The Word of God speaks much more and diversely about all these things than are contained in the Reformed Creeds. The latter express an Evangelical-Catholic minimum, but not the Catholic maximum. However, this "more and diverse" is revealed in our time as Catholic truth in the New Testament, which will be dealt with in the following chapters.

Isolated Evangelical principles or theories were exalted to the level of a Catholic article of faith and soon developed into doctrines that were heretical for those who professed them and destructively detrimental to the Church. In Evangelical belief and theology these principles were established and regarded as sufficient. Millions of Evangelical Christians no longer have Reformed-Catholic or common Christian conceptions in mind when they speak of the Church, forgiveness, redemption, holy communion, the Last Judgment, baptism and eternal life. They are merely mouthing the remains of Christian terminology. This is not in any sense because of a lack of piety. But "Evangelical" Protestantism simply disintegrates if (to use Kierkegaard's distinction), it claims to be a "norm" or uniquely valid principle of the Church's faith and doctrine instead of accepting its proper role as the corrective of a Catholic substance originally given and received. It is only upon the fertile soil of Catholicism that Evangelical Protestantism has any right of existence or any future at all. This is the divine significance of the "Catholic revelations" in the New Testament, and theological science among Evangelical Protestants of our time must cope with these Catholic truths. There will have to be a re-statement of our Evangelical Protestant position from the standpoint of a Catholic orientation.

Catholic fulfillment of Evangelical doctrine is therefore something wholly other than the mere addition of a few "Catholic" ideas to the traditional content of Evangelical beliefs. When we speak of the Catholic fulfillment of our Protestant conceptions of Evangelical truth, we mean that we are under a holy compulsion of the Spirit and Word of God to believe as Evangelical Catholics and to take our stand in witnessing for the same faith as our separated brethren so that, circumstances permitting, and to the surprise of both sides, a wholly new Catholic thought and outlook may arise.

The Catholic fulfillment of our Evangelical mission to the Catholic mother church, which still remains unfinished, is therefore essential to our witness. We also believe that we must point out certain juridical, monarchical, Mariological and ecclesiological aspects of Roman Catholicism since the Reformation era which stand in need of our Evangelical Catholic corrective if Catholic unity is ever to be re-established. Certain Catholic truths of central importance are somehow schematized and rationalized in Roman Catholic practice and theory, and consequently are petrified in the concept and form of a human system, and also in the rigid structure of an historical mode. Consequently, these authentic Catholic principles are in danger of being changed from a uniting and constructive *pneumatikon* into a human and earthly *idea* that is detrimental and even ruinous to Catholicity. What is

meant here in general and in particular will be clarified
in the following contrasts.

We say *Yes* to tradition and *No* to traditionalism. *Yes*
to the office of the pope, and *No* to papalism. *Yes* to the
canon law of the church, *No* to legalism. To Mary the
most blessed Mother of God we say *Yes!* But we must say
No to Marianism! *Yes* to the institution of the Church,
and to episcopacy, confession, etc., but *No* to institution-
alism. *Yes* to the abundant grace of the holy sacraments
and to the sacramental character of the Church; *No* to
sacramentalism. *Yes* to Rome as the central See, but *No*
to centralism and Romanism. We know from conversations with Catholics whose witness is reliable, and (to mention only one literary example) from reading the French
priest's diary of Ignace Lepp, *"Motes and Beams,"* on the
offenses and scandals of a Christian world, that Roman
Catholic excesses which are at variance with early Catholic
and biblical principles of revelation are also recognized
by many Catholics. They become increasingly aware that
"Christians separated from Rome are not entirely in error
and that the Church must acknowledge her own mistakes
in order to make the reunion of Christians possible" (*op.
cit.*, p. 186).

These excesses of the system, whose origin may be
sought just as surely in the early Middle Ages as in the
centuries of the Counter-Reformation, have certainly not
all become equally important and dangerous. Some of
them are simply expressions of Catholic piety or clerical
practice which have never been defended or advocated
in any specific theological thesis. As a matter of fact, however, there have always been, and must always be, various
"heresies" within the Church—in spite of the vigilance of

the supreme teaching office!—and it is possible that in these unauthorized but actual "excesses" something of the latent, nameless infirmity inherent in the very life of the Church becomes apparent. Karl Rahner [33] has characterized these excesses as a modern type of "cryptogamous heresy." A heresy of this kind is never set forth in theological terms or defined as official doctrine, but it does find expression in the reality of the Church's life and undermines its Catholic and Apostolic character.

Other "excesses" on the other hand have assumed the fixed form of dogmatic decisions and practices, as for example the definition of papal *ex cathedra* pronouncements as irreformable *ex sese non ex consensu ecclesiae,** or the decisive importance of the Church's "pious opinion" when a dogma is formally defined, as in the case of the bodily Assumption of Mary into heaven. In such instances it seems to us that there is a doctrinal development which exceeds the proper limits of a Christian and Catholic theology. It is, after all, a characteristic of real theology never to make inferences of this kind. We can doubtless say too little, but we can also say too much in our theology.

---

[33] Karl Rahner, *Gefahren im heutigen Katholizismus*, 1950, p. 69.

* Catholic theologians object to Evangelical criticism of this Vatican formula (Denzinger No. 1839). Of course there is no Protestant opposition to irreformable papal decisions in matters of faith which are in accord with the necessary *consensus ecclesiae*. The pope may and should make use of his supreme teaching authority only as a member of the Body of Christ (even though he is the most pre-eminent member!), i.e. within the spiritual communion of the whole Church and of all his fellow-bishops. This formula, originating in the religious and cultural milieu of the 19th century was meant merely to declare that the authority of the pope to make an irreformable, *ex cathedra* decision was not based on the consensus of the Church but on the position and mandate of the pope as the Vicar of Christ. The wording may refer to the papal *auctoritas* of the doctrinal definition, "per assistentiam divinam ipsi in beato Petro promissam" rather than the origin of the matter of the dogma. We should give serious consideration to this interpretation.

In either case the Catholic equilibrium of the Church is disturbed.

When speaking of Evangelical desires for reform, Catholic theologians still like to explain that a "Evangelical" reformation of the Church, if it is really necessary at all, can never come "from outside" but only from within the Church itself. They point out that the Council of Trent and many post-Reformation popes have undertaken and accomplished authentic evangelical reforms with outstanding success.

But we can only ask with bewilderment whether the call to Reformation came entirely "from outside," and we can only wonder what could have been the source and origin of the reform movement of the Cistercians, and the call of St. Francis and of St. Catherine, if not from within the Catholic Church. Was it not through Catholic monks and priests that the call of the Holy Spirit went out to the Church? Why do responsible churchmen and theologians of the Roman Church still give so little consideration to the theology of Martin Luther and the Augsburg Confession, which was certainly a call "from within" to all members of the Church everywhere? It is fortunate for men of our time that the following voice of French Catholicism can be heard in regard to the relationship of the Catholic Church to the modern ecumenical movement: "To speak frankly, we do not realize the profundity, nor do we know the exact significance of the question which Our Lord has posed to the Church through the ecumenical movement. We shall discover its meaning in our readiness to learn from reality, and in a brotherly and objective hearing of the aims and desires of our separated brethren, in fidelity to Our Lord and to His Church. We must be closer to our brethren in order to understand the call which Our Lord is addressing to them and which He is directing toward ourselves through these same brethren. We must prepare a place for them in our hearts and in our highest thinking, in order that we may be able to help them exactly in the situation where they actually find themselves here and now, and nowhere else. . . . The ecumenical movement therefore voices the call of God, and the Church must not even dare to think of ignoring it." In this statement we believe that we have found an authentic Catholic effort to attain both theologically and ecclesiastically to a "vision of the mystery of the Church that will embrace all of the separated communions inclusively." [33a] We Lutherans are waiting eagerly for this vision. Regardless of our right to speak "from outside" since the Reformation movement broke with the papacy and separated from the Catholic communion of altar and liturgy, would not our Catholic brethren and the earthly head of the Church be more readily attentive to our "Evangelical ideals and concerns" if the lost Catholic principles of Catholic life were again discovered and accepted among us, and if Evangelical Christians made it known that their *contra* is to be understood only as proceeding from a profound Catholic Christian *with and for* the Church of Rome? That would be the real beginning of the Catholic fulfillment of our Evangelical mission to the Mother Church.

Except as the beginning of a Catholic discovery of Evangelical Christianity, how else can we interpret the remarkable statement of the Dominican, M. J. Le Guillou, who concludes his article, previously cited, with the following comment: "that which divides us unequivocally (the question of the primacy) does not enter into the question of what we possess in common in ecclesiology. For them, as

[33a] M. J. Le Guillou, O.P. in *Revue Istina*, 1956, No. 4, pp. 416-442.

for ourselves . . . . the Church is the Body of Christ in the Pauline sense of the term. . . . for them, as for ourselves, the Church is a sacramental mystery in which the role of the historical institution is always clearly understood in its true significance. For them, as for ourselves, Christ is the sacramental sign, the selfsame Christ who lived and labored visibly among men, and now forevermore in His glory continues His mission through the Church as an institution. For them, as for ourselves, there is an indissoluble unity of Word and sacrament, and the Church is to be found only where there is historical continuity through which the Church's apostolicity is manifested. We have the same conceptions of the visible components of the Church's unity. For them, as for ourselves, it is a question of unity in faith, membership in a unique, sacramental and hierarchical structure, and common partaking of the same sacraments, especially the holy Eucharist."

We must give due praise to the theological achievements and ecclesiastical decisions of the Council of Trent! Adolph von Harnack did not exaggerate when he expressed the opinion that the division of the Church could have been avoided if the Council of Trent had been held only a few decades earlier. However, modern Catholic scholars frankly admit that "there was no one at the Council who, being sympathetic in his feelings for Luther, could even approximately understand his disputatious and yet deeply religious personality." [34] Consequently, there have been many who "possess no authentic knowledge of Luther" and who do not see "that the problem of Luther is still with us and makes a further development

[34] Adolph Stakemeier, *Das Konzil von Trient über die Heilsgewissheit* 1947, p. 83.

of Catholic theology indispensable." [35] But Luther's theology must doubtless still be first approached through Catholic theology.

In the course of the controversy with the Church, Luther's statements certainly assumed the form of a very antithetical, anti-Catholic accentuation, and consequently the content of truth in his message, derived from the Holy Spirit, has been increasingly overshadowed by the polemical defiance and renunciation of Roman tradition. It may be psychologically intelligible but it is nevertheless a great misfortune for the Church everywhere (as a participant of the Council of Trent regretfully remarked in regard to the problem of the assurance of salvation), that "the Council dismissed Luther's opinion without any knowledge of his arguments." [36] We feel that it would now be an appropriate time for our Roman brethren to acknowledge that the "case of Luther" was by no means settled by the canons of the Council of Trent.

We should not be offended by any Catholic, however, who possesses absolutely no understanding of the usual Protestant *"No!"* to the veneration of Mary, or to the Pope, the sacrifice of the Mass, Confession and canon law. Catholics feel that a great deal of this Evangelical negation would be destructive of Christianity rather than serve as a reforming or purifying principle for Catholicism. But we believe that the time is near when our fellow-Christians of the Catholic Church may be certain that the Evangelical mission has no intention of depriving them of the veneration of Mary, the divine ordinance of Confession, the excellence of the Mass, or the supreme pastoral and teaching office instituted by Jesus Christ. It seeks instead to bring

35 *Op. cit.,* p. 79.
36 *Op. cit.,* p. 88.

all of this heritage to an Evangelical-Catholic fulfillment
and to an even richer development, and to purify all of
these things from un-Catholic distortions. There is a Evangelical *protest* which properly aims at a positive witness
for the life of the world-wide Catholic Church.

This positive witness may still make various demands
that are difficult for the Roman Catholic Church of our
time. Evangelical doctrinal truth, even with its neo-Cath-
olic orientation in the present century, will make it as
hard for the Catholic Church to accept our positive witness as Catholic truths have made its acceptance easier
for us Lutherans. However, this is not wholly the responsibility of men but is rather the inexorable will and integrity
of the Holy Spirit at work within His Church. God always requires something of us when His grace reforms us.

The Spirit of Truth can still make *one* out of two, even
in our day and age, just as He once performed the miracle
of making *one* people out of Gentiles and Jews (Eph. 2:14).
The Catholic fulfillment of our Evangelical mission, as
can already be seen now and then in the blessed signs of
our own time, could even perform the miracle of making
our Evangelical witness and mission a *Catholic* (and therefore binding) message which Roman Catholics would
acknowledge and accept, and there would be once again
only *one* fold under the *one* shepherd, gathered together
in the communion of the *one* altar.

It was a noble Evangelical endeavor of this kind that
Martin Luther had hoped to accomplish for the Catholic
Church, "the Bride entrusted to the Lord." In this task
we should be his willing collaborators and followers.

ERNST FINCKE

CATHOLIC TRUTH
IN THE NEW TESTAMENT

I. THE LIFE OF THE CHURCH

1. The Signal

a) *The Situation*

Evangelical Christianity is now facing the most difficult decision in its history. An indication of this situation is the fact that Evangelical theology of the present time is simply taking it for granted that the New Testament contains a more or less considerable number of so-called Catholic terms and ideas which contradict fundamental Evangelical principles. *"The time when we could contrast scripture as a whole with Catholicism would seem to be irretrievably past,"* because "the canon of the New Testament allows a real place and basis for early Catholicism" as Ernst Käsemann [1] has pointed out. It was the historical school of religion that first propounded this point of view. In 1880, writing about the pastoral epistles,[2] Holtzmann commented, "They contain the whole of Catholicity *in nuce*." In 1897, Wernle said, "We are blind to everything Catholic in the writings of Paul." [3] Church historians then discovered the close connection between the New Testament and the be-

---

1 Käsemann, E., in *"Evangelische Theologie"* 1951-52, 19.
2 Holtzmann, H. J., *"Pastoralbriefe"* (Timothy and Titus), 1880, 227.
3 Wernle, P., *Der Christ und die Sünde*, 1897, 18.

113

ginnings of the Catholic Church. In the opinion of Rudolph Sohm,[4] "The Catholicism of the ancient Church is the direct continuation of early Christianity." Both Harnack [5] and Holl [6] were in agreement with this opinion. There were, moreover, the comments of Schlatter, the great Biblicist, still given but little consideration,[7] on the profound difference between Reformation and biblical conceptions [8] which led his student, Althaus, to side with Luther against Paul on many points,[9] and to demand a "Evangelical scriptural criticism of Jewish thought in the New Testament." [10] This kind of thinking was carried to even greater lengths. Emil Brunner could only defend his famous concept of the Church by frankly admitting that a different idea, which he attacked as erroneous, could nevertheless be "found in the New Testament." [11] In a report on the point of view of the Lutheran World Federation concerning the question of women, it was said that we must "argue" differently than Paul in I Cor. 11 and I Tim. 2:14, because "he does not attain to the full height of the gospel in these passages." [12] As a result of New Testament critical studies in recent years, Käsemann charges that Luke "is not a later disciple of Paul, but the first representative of primitive Catholicism." [13]

4 Sohm, R., *Das altkatolische Kirchenrecht und das Dekret Gratians,* 1918, 65.

5 Harnack, A., *Kirchenverfassung* . . . . referring to the first two centuries of the Christian Era, 1910, 119.

6 Holl, K., *Gesammelte Aufsätze* II, 44 ff.

7 Käsemann, E., *Theologie und Kirche,* in *Zeitschrift,* 1957, 4.

8 Schlatter, A., especially see *Luthers Deutung des Römerbriefs,* 1917.

9 Althaus, P., *Paulus und Luther über den Menschen,* 1951, 95 et al.

10 Althaus, P., *Die christliche Wahrheit,* II, 301.

11 Brunner, E., *Das Missverständnis der Kirche,* 1951, 31, 29, 73, 78 ff.

12 Hahn, E., *Partnerschaft,* 1952, 54 f.

13 Käsemann, E., *Neutestamentliche Fragen heute* in *Evangelische Theologie,* 1957, 20.

b) *The Judgment*

In the light of these developments, the Evangelical Churches must now decide whether they can any longer assume that "the partial teachings of the Reformation should be considered as the whole of the Christian gospel" [14] or accord a greater authority to Holy Scripture in its entirety.[15] Generally speaking, it has been customary to decide in favor of the first possibility, basing our decision upon the following argument that is both significant and far-reaching: the Gospel was a protest against the tendency of natural man, particularly apparent in official Judaism, and never wholly renounced by biblical authors, to lay hold of God, confining Him "legally" [16] within an "infallible" canon and a uniquely authoritative doctrine and philosophy, while making Him accessible only through a sacral, ecclesiastical institution sharply distinguished from the world. This theory would mean that the fact of the gospel was really a secular event and consequently it should be treated like something pertaining to this present world. Consequently, we now find it necessary to subordinate Holy Scripture to a criticism of its message.[17] We are convinced that it is precisely because of this differentiation in regard to the Word of God, and the attempts to correct Holy Scripture, that God is somehow disposed of, and His Word is superseded by the opinions of men even as the whole of Christian life is secularized in the very likeness of the world. We also believe that the idea of an "apostasy from the pure gospel" even within the New Testament

14 Dilschneider, O.A., *Gefesselte Kirche,* 1953, 45.
15 Paul Schütz in the *Deutschen Pfarrerblatt,* Vol. 1, 9, 1952.
16 Käsemann, E., in *Evangelische Theologie,* 1951-52, 21.
17 Diem, Hermann, in *Dogmatik 1955.*

itself cannot be considered as purely historical,[18] for *the
apparent contradiction in the New Testament really constitutes an indissoluble unity*. It is only the acknowledgement of this unity which can protect the Church, whether
Roman or Protestant, from secularization. It might be
well, in the following section, for us to consider this contradiction, although it does not admit of an easy explanation.

2. The apparent contradiction in the New Testament

a) *The Gospel*

"The poor have the gospel preached to them" (Mt. 11:5;
Lk. 4:18). In this passage Jesus uses an expression which
He regarded as especially characteristic of the Old Testament (Is. 40:9 and elsewhere). The *Gospel,* which He was
to proclaim, was the good news that the salvation of the
poor had already come to pass. This was precisely the message that had never been heard before, both gladdening
and angering the hearts of men by its coming, and revealing that instead of an immediate increase of their religious
knowledge and quality, Jesus was mediating the wonderful
tidings to the poor that salvation had already been won for
them through a blessed event that far surpassed their own
potentialities. It was this event which was itself the gospel,
the coming of the Messias into the world of the poor, in
their own flesh and their own condition. And furthermore
the hearing of this gospel is revealed as a very part of the
blessed act of redemption: "he who hears my word, and
believes . . . . has passed from death to life" (Jn. 5:24).
This "life" however is not the end of our spiritual poverty
(Mt. 5:3) but means that we shall become ever poorer

---

[18] Siehe Wilh. Kamlah, *Christentum und Geschichtlichkeit,* 1951, 67 f.

within ourselves, "not having a justice of my own" (Phil. 3:8), becoming "little children" (Mt. 18:3), and practicing self-denial (Mt. 16:24). The gospel therefore stands in opposition to the religion of the Law and all natural religion. In this respect it is essentially something distinctive which we can show forth in the special knowledge, the particular effect, the unique merit, the peculiar quality or technique of worship conducted by men, a holy order in which we can become obedient to the law of God. However, those who receive the gospel know that they are the poor to whom the unsurpassed and equal dignity of kinship with God has been bequeathed in Christ alone.

b) *The so-called "Catholic Line" in the New Testament*

The gospel proclaims salvation for "the poor" who possess nothing which they can bring before God. Nevertheless, in Acts 10:35 it is said, "he who fears him and does what is right is acceptable to him" and according to 10:31, Cornelius finds the way to salvation because his "alms have been remembered." Christ's statements about reward are surprisingly frequent also: Mt. 16:27 on the rewarding of our deeds; 12:36 concerning the things we say; 6:3 and 6:18 on the merit for alms-giving, prayer and fasting; Mt. 5:11 and Lk. 6:35 on the "great" reward for suffering persecution and for loving our enemies. Some years ago the relation of the idea of merit to the gospel was elucidated by Bornkamm in a book that was highly regarded.[19] However, it was not sufficiently noted that a merit, apparently contrary to Mt. 20:14, must always be expressly in proportion to the act performed (Mt. 25:14 ff; Lk. 6:38; I Cor. 3:8), and that Jesus, like Paul in I Cor. 3:8, says that any-

19 Bornkamm, G., *Der Lohngedanke im Neuen Testament,* 1947.

one whose good works are done merely to be seen of men
will *not* lose his reward (Mt. 10:42) but will certainly lose
the greater reward (Mt. 6:2, 5) which the epistle to the
Hebrews (6:10) attributes to the justice of God. Jesus and
the Apostles never hesitated to make use of typical expressions of the Jewish doctrine of merit which were sayings
taken from the "accumulated capital" constituting "a good
foundation against the time to come, in order that they
may lay hold on the true life" (Lk. 12:33; 18:22; I Tim.
6:19),[20] or the saying in Apoc. 14:13 [21] that "their works
follow them" (in the life to come) to which is related the
idea that "the fine linen" of the heavenly spouse "is the
just deeds of the saints" (Apoc. 19:8).[22] This apparent contradiction in the gospel becomes particularly noticeable
when the New Testament uses a passage from Tobias 4:9
in commending charity because it "covers a multitude of
sins" completely effacing them (I Pet. 4:8; Jas. 5:20).[23]
This same idea is made concrete in I Tim. 2:15, which
tells us that "women will be saved by childbearing (and
rearing) if they continue in faith and love." However, was
it not Jesus Himself who defined works of love as the test
for all men at the Last Judgment (Mt. 25:40), and the
"love of the sinful woman as the means whereby she received forgiveness" as Schlatter remarked in regard to Lk.
7:47. Our human efforts for our own salvation seem to
acquire an importance which somehow limits Christ's
unique act of redemption, and we now find another series
of passages according to which man's existence and activity
also possess real significance for the salvation of others,
analogous to the work of Christ. First of all we may quote

20 Strack-Billerbeck, *Kommentar zum Neuen Testament*, III, 655, 817.
21 *Theologisches Wörterbuch zum Neuen Testament*, II, 645, 6.
22 *Theologisches Wörterbuch zum Neuen Testament*, II, 226, 25.
23 *Theologisches Wörterbuch zum Neuen Testament*, III, 559 f.

from Mt. 10:41, with reference to Schlatter's commentary, "He who receives a prophet because he is a prophet, shall receive a prophet's reward, and he who receives a just man (in times of persecution), because he is a just man, shall receive a just man's reward." At this point we become aware of man's obligation to God to make himself responsible for another's welfare, an idea which is frequently found in the teaching of Jesus. The peace of the disciple comes upon the household that receives the disciple (Mt. 10:13), and consequently, when the father of a family makes the decision, it will determine the salvation or condemnation of all the members of his household. The faith of those who carried the man sick of the palsy to Jesus made it possible for Him to impart forgiveness to the sick man (Mt. 9:2), and friends will receive their benefactor "into the everlasting dwellings" (Lk. 16:9). But all of this comes within the scope of God's purpose, who will impart His blessings not only directly, but also through the agency of men. Jesus acted in accordance with this principle when He left an authority like His own to the Church and to certain of her members: "whose sins you shall forgive (not merely telling of forgiveness), they are forgiven them" (Jn. 20:23). According to Mt. 9:8, God gave such power not only to Christ but also "to men." Thus Christ gave the disciples collectively (Mt. 18:1, 18) and Peter individually (Mt. 16:19) the authority and mandate "to bind" (i.e. to expel) and "to loose" every sinner so that his very relationship with God "in heaven" and his eternal existence are at stake.[24] In accordance with the passage in Deut. 12:12, there seems to be an emphasis in Acts 8:20 ff. upon this

---

[24] *Theologisches Wörterbuch zum Neuen Testament,* I, 60; and also: Strack-Billerbeck, *Komm.* I, 738.

expelling "power of the Apostles' word" [25] and on the strength of this mandate the Apostle Paul claims that a member of the Church should be excommunicated in order that he may be in lesser danger of eternal judgment (I Cor. 5:5). This is the same Christ-like authority whereby the Holy Spirit, still blowing where He will, is mediated by the Apostles to everyone "through the laying on of the apostles' hands" (Acts 8:17 f. and Tim. 1:6).

3. The Catholic Character of the Gospel

We must now face the task of harmonizing the apparent contradictions in the New Testament in such a way that they will not tend to mutual debasement or suppression. The so-called "Catholic line" may no longer be regarded as a disturbing, marginal phenomenon which we should at best ignore, but is instead a clear indication that the gospel itself possesses a Catholic character. The significance of this fact will be explained in the rest of this chapter. We may begin with a statement of Adolph Schlatter in which he sums up his criticism of Reformation thought entirely from a New Testament point of view: "Luther invariably based his judgments upon the assumption that whatever we are and whatever we do *either* proceeds from grace *or* from ourselves alone. *The idea of creation is totally lacking in this kind of judgment.*" [26] In other words, Schlatter believes that we may perceive a contradiction between various bible passages which attribute everything to the grace of Christ and other passages which lay stress upon the importance of human action and being, simply because we do not sufficiently understand the nature of

25 Hänchen, E., *Kommentar zur Apostelgeschichte,* p. 262.
26 Schlatter, A., *Luthers Deutung des Römerbriefs,* 1917, 85 f.

creation. If we could think of creation and salvation in such a way that the full importance of both would be preserved, our conception would be genuinely Catholic, i.e. it would be complete.

a) *Creation, God, Christ*

The nature of creation is such that *God wills to do nothing alone, although He governs and sustains everything unceasingly.* The mysterious relation between grace and our own action is therefore of great importance in creation, as is also the possibility of demoniacal independence and self-worship. God gives physical nature autonomous ordinances and laws in such measure that it becomes possible for us to worship them instead of Him. He gives the angels a status of such kind that His own life and action become fully apparent and effectual in them (Gen. 16:13; Apoc. 12:7). There are many kinds of fatherhood in heaven and on earth, although there is only one Father from whom all fatherhood derives its name, i.e. its very existence (Eph. 3:14). It is the nature of creation to exist wholly *through* God and nevertheless *with* God. This becomes evident, for instance, in the mystery of justice and judgment which "are the establishment of his throne" (Ps. 96:2 Douay version or Ps. 97:2), as if they were a separate reality. We see it again in the mystery of marriage in which a most human relationship is confirmed by the unity of God's eternal bond, and in the mystery of all nature-symbolism through which it becomes possible to lift up "my eyes to the mountains, from whence help shall come to me" (Ps. 120:1 Douay version, or Ps. 121:1). It is apparent in the mystery of the "numinous power of things" without whose "sacral quality" there could be no worship at all,[27] and finally, in the mystery of sacrifices which, in the Bible, appear quite self-evidently as a given condition of creation, of immense importance to the world of men and of angels, and whose influence upon God's own course of action is described in a very striking way, as for instance in Genesis 8:21. Since everything originally emerged into full reality in Christ, it should not be supposed that Christ came among us as a substitute for creation, for although He came down into the world from above, He was nevertheless to become the promised seed of Eve (Gen. 3:15) and of Abraham, and to be the son of David and of Mary. In His whole life and work He was always obedient to the faith of Abraham, David, Mary and all His predecessors and ancestors. He was sent to bless His people (Acts 3:26) and to govern them as the "Anointed" of God, to pray for His own as their High Priest. But He was able to do all of this only because it is really possible in creation for a man to bless others and govern them as one "anointed" (Is. 45:1) and to make effectual intercession for them "through his own righteousness" (Ezech. 14:4; Job 42:8). We may say that Christ was primarily sent to make atonement for the world. However, according to Isaias (53:12), can true intercession ever be anything other than propitiatory atonement? Was not God earnestly seeking someone among men who would "stand in the gap" (Ezech. 22:30) against His wrath? We may ask if primitive Christianity was unwilling to accept as God's Word the saying of the Jewish martyr, "But in me and in my brethren the wrath of the Almighty . . . shall cease" (II Mac. 7:38). God creates and sustains all things alone and yet always in conjunction with His creatures. This truth is also pertinent to the work of salvation. Christ is

27 Tillich, P., *Religiöse Verwirklichung*, 1930, 164.

the only savior, but always in union with His human brethren. The "Son of Man" comes from above "with the clouds of heaven" but He is nevertheless visible prophetically in "the people of the saints of the most High" (Dan. 7:13 and 27).

b) *Christ, Creation, and the Church*

In any case we are now faced with the unequivocal decision either to build upon the "elements of the world" or upon Christ (Gal. 4:3, 9; Col. 2:8, 20). Anyone who is "in Christ" as the result of this decision is a "new creature" (II Cor. 5:17). The new creation, however, does not take the place of the older, but is rather its completion and perfection. But what does this really mean? Through the instrumentality of three "elements of the world" God had made Israel a special possession of His own. It was through the blood covenant with Abraham that the Israelites became a chosen people. God was present among them in their religious rites. They were bound to Himself as the Lord through the all-inclusive Law. Everything pointed to salvation, and strangely enough, to salvation from the Law. For the Law, itself an indispensable complement of the filial adoption of Abraham and of the religious rites, made faith in the election and in God's ritual presence illusory because it was necessary to anathematize anyone who did not observe the Law completely (Gal. 3:10). Paul, who at one time willingly observed the whole Law as a Pharisee,[28] not merely for his own sake but for Israel's also, perceived that the true Israel, the incontestable Election, the consummation of justice and righteousness, and

---

28 Lohmeyer, E., *Grundprobleme paulinischer Theologie,* 1929, 92.

the whole divine economy, had come into being through the vicarious, messianic events of the crucifixion and the resurrection of Jesus. It would be impossible and unthinkable, of course, that anything in creation itself could serve as a vicarious representative in this way. The Law, and likewise all the "elements of the world" have, so to speak, surrendered their immediate religious significance to Christ. The old Adam, definitely and manifestly, has become fixed in his anti-godliness. The way has therefore been opened to "faith" and to "life in Christ."

This "life in Christ" however is no mere tranquil existence, but a movement, a divine dynamic, "from faith unto faith" (Rom. 1:16 f), from the resurrection of Christ until the general resurrection (Rom. 8:11). It is a saying *yes* to being which has been given to us (Phil. 3:12), an impulse of the Holy Spirit (Rom. 8:14) and of the love of Christ (II Cor. 5:14). Our "life in Christ" obliges us to "walk in Christ" (Col. 2:6). It is a way that leads from justification through Christ upon the Cross to our justification in His presence on the Last Day (I Cor. 4:4). It is a preparatory process that continues "until Christ is formed in you" (Gal. 4:19). The preaching of the gospel will be fulfilled in the obedience of the nations (Rom. 15:16 ff.); the sufferings of Christ will be completed by the sufferings of Christians (Col. 1:24). This activity of the Christian life is not to be considered as merely an effect of the act of redemption, but rather as a very part of redemption itself. It is God's work (Phil. 1:6; 2:12), in which, with enormous responsibility, all of us are to participate "with fear and trembling." To sum up, the idea of creation which conceives of Almighty God as allowing the creature to share in His work, and the cosmic law which ordains that "what a man sows, that he will also reap" (Gal. 6:7) are also relevant to the matter of our salvation.

Properly speaking, it is a question of what must still be accomplished in Christ, a unique work "for building up the body of Christ" (Eph. 4:12, 16). This word *body* [29] used by Jesus Himself, brings the *unity* of the whole economy of salvation into view. We see the unity of the vicarious events of the crucifixion and resurrection with the present life of the Church, and the unity of the present time with the future consummation. We perceive the unity of the individual Christian with the communion of the Saints, and the unity of Christ and the Church, the unity of the inward and spiritual with the outward and visible. *In this Body of Christ the old and the new creation is both united and distinguished.* We shall consider first the unity and then the distinction.

The physical body of Christ is a part of the material creation and at the same time a spiritual reality, the beginning of the new creation. According to the testimony of the New Testament, the Church of Christ is not merely figurative but is actually the same body of Christ which was sacrificed on the Cross because Christ the King incorporates His people into Himself. Consequently the Church is the beginning of the new creation but is nevertheless a part of an historically visible, sociologically and essentially concrete, earthly reality. Therefore, in the choice of the Twelve, to whom was committed the judging of the eternal and glorified Israel (Mt. 19:28), we are to see the administration of the primitive Church in a very concrete manner.[30] Likewise, in *Baptism* we see the sac-

[29] Hahn, W., *Gottesdienst und Opfer Christi*, 1951, 51 ff.
[30] Bultmann, R., *Theologie des Neuen Testaments*, 1954, 60. Campenhausen, v. H., *Kirchliches Amt. . . . ,* 1953, 16

rifice of Christ and the liturgical and canonical act of the Church as the foundation of our "life in Christ," the new creation. Moreover, we note the Apostle Paul's personal conviction that all the goodness he found in his churches was intended for his own "crown of glory" at the Last Day [31] (II Cor. 1:14; Phil. 2:16; I Thess. 2:19). He himself will then also become the "glory" of these same churches (II Cor. 1:14), and in his own life nothing occurred, nor was there any personal suffering, which would not be of importance to them (Col. 1:24; II Tim. 2:10; II Cor. 4:12). This was only possible because his personal relationship with the churches was like the relationship of Christ with the whole Church everywhere. Finally, the inward and spiritual and the outward and visible unity of the Church are necessarily concomitant in the Body of Christ. This was convincingly shown by the two journeys which the Apostle Paul made to Jerusalem. In regard to one of these journeys, he commented (Gal. 2:2): "I conferred with them on the gospel which I preach among the Gentiles, but separately with the men of authority; lest perhaps I should be running, or had run in vain." This could only mean that his preaching of the gospel, for which he had received a direct mandate from God, and through which a flourishing, spiritual life had developed, would be futile and senseless without the concurrence of these men in Jerusalem or apart from the doctrinal unity of the whole Church. The other journey was undertaken to bring the collection to Jerusalem (II Cor. 8-9; Rom. 15:25 ff.; Acts 20:22 ff.). It was not only an act of love but also an "act of Faith," [32] an affirmation and confirmation of visible unity with the primitive Church and the universal Church, for

[31] Lohmeyer, E., *op. cit.*, 195 ff.
[32] Bultmann, R., *Theologie des Neuen Testaments,* 1954, 62.

which Paul was prepared "to sacrifice his labors, his freedom and even his life." [33]

The Body of Christ is just as visible as the earthly creation, but this visibleness is of another kind. It is sacramental. The word *sacramental* has but recently been revived in connection with the idea of the Church as the Body of Christ. In this respect, however, it is said that "we must understand the Church in accordance with the analogy of baptism and Last Supper" (Karl Barth, *Dogm.* I, 2, 253). We would do well, however, in considering this mystery, not to begin with this particular sacramental symbolism as was done by Barth and others. For otherwise the symbolism of the Old and New Testaments would be placed at the same level to an excessive degree. Rather, in view of the abundant history of the term "sacramentum-mysterium" we should begin with the accentuation which Jesus gave this term when He spoke of the "mystery of the Kingdom of God" (Mk. 4:11). Jesus meant that the coming Kingdom of God was secretly present already, hidden in His person and His sacrifice. When the Church is called His Body, it now means above all else that in her visible aspect we see the representation of both the past events of Christ's life and the glory that is to be revealed. This visibleness, however, does not possess an intrinsic significance like the visibleness of natural creation, but it signifies and effects the wholly invisible presence, here and now, of divine salvation and glory, and impels us to seek it in faithful devotedness and to expect it in confident hope.[34]

33 Schlatter, A., *Geschichte der ersten Christenheit,* 1926, 243.
34 Van d. Leeuw, G., *Sakramentstheologie, Nijkerk,* 1949, 139.

c) *Catholic Particularity*

It has been said that we should consider the Church as a whole in a sacramental manner, but it is precisely because of her outward and visible aspect that there must also be sacraments in the *particular* and proper sense of the term. It is a universal structural law of the Church that we must now consider, the law of particularity or concreteness. In a recently published book [35] this "tendency to concreteness" was designated as something that is typically Roman. However, it could be said in reply that it is also something very typical of the New Testament itself which the Roman Church is seeking to uphold and maintain, even if not always in forms that could be vindicated by an appeal to the New Testament. This law of particularity was especially evident in the choice of the twelve apostles, for in them it was displayed in an exemplary, concrete and visible manner, making it possible to realize the nature of the Church as a whole in all its power and fulness. What is the Lord's Supper if not a concrete realization of something that is always present in the Church? Or let us consider another example: in the Apocalypse of John the martyrs appear as exemplary Christians in their witness (Apoc. 12:11) and they are mentioned together with the "prophets" and the "saints" as distinguished from the faithful in general (Apoc. 11:18; 18:24).[36] We find the same thing in Paul, for although he speaks of all Christians as "saints" he does not hesitate to use this term in a special sense when he refers to the apostles and prophets (Eph. 3:5). In regard to this, Käsemann says, "Between the Head and the Body there is an interposition of

---

[35] Grünewald, H., *Römische und pneumatische Katolizität*, 1956.
[36] Fascher, E., *Prophetes*, 1927, 186; K. Holl, Ges. Aufsätze II, 68 ff.

chosen and favored individuals on account of their charismatic gifts." [37] The law of particularity is also apparent in references to the city of Jerusalem. Christians continue to think of it as the "Holy City" (Mt. 27:53), and the whole Church often seems to be like an extension of this one particular community of "saints" (II Cor. 9:12; Eph. 2:19). Finally, the "Gospel" is made concrete in certain distinctive passages (see I Cor. 15:1 ff.) and "there has never been an *euanggelion* without (this) *paradosis*." [38] In brief, *particularity belongs to the very nature of the Church; it is implicit in the word "Catholic" which, for this very reason, cannot be translated.* For this word does not only mean "universal" or "general" but also, according to Aristotle, it has reference to something which "contains the whole in a particular part." [39]

d) *Catholic Polarity*

There is nevertheless a great danger that particularity may lead to a false concreteness and legalism, or more briefly to secularization of the gospel. The Church avoids this danger only when she is mindful of *the polar tension* which, according to the New Testament, is the dominant factor in this particularity. The most striking example would be the relationship which existed between the apostle Paul and the Twelve. He knew that his own status was similar to theirs, but not as the thirteenth among them. We find an unbalanced juxtaposition of the authoritative office belonging to the Twelve and the charismata of St. Paul. The one was necessarily subordinate to

37 Käsemann, E., *Leib und Leib Christi,* 1933, 146; and D. Bonhoeffer, *Ethik,* 1949, p. 11.
38 Bultmann, R., *Theologie des Neuen Testaments,* 1954, 444.
39 Aristotle, *Metaphysics,* 26.

the other and pointed beyond itself to the Lord of the Church and to her invisible, eternal reality.[40] Similarly, we find an inabrogable relationship of polarity between the authority of the apostle Peter (Mt. 16:18) and the rest of the disciples (Mt. 18:18), as between the leader of a Church and the ecclesiastical community (II Cor. 7:15 and 1:24).[41] We note the relationship between the mystery of matrimony (Eph. 5:23 ff.) and celibacy (Mt. 19:12), the second birth of Baptism (Titus 3:5) and the Word (I Pet. 1:23), the idea of grace as divine favor (Rom. 3:24) and as something administered by men (I Pet. 4:10).[42] In all areas of the Christian life there is found this same enormous and *unequal tension between the more concrete and the more universal*. The one always points to the other and beyond itself to the only abiding reality, the Lord and the life to come. We can never say that the one *or* the other aspect is more essential, as for instance in speaking of the clergy *or* the faithful, law *or* love, the sacraments *or* the Word. Whenever this has occurred, whether in the Roman Catholic over-emphasis of the objective and concrete, or in the Protestant exaggeration of the subjective and universal, it has been detrimental to the mystery of the Church and to her sacramental character and Catholicity, with the result that the Church has then appeared before men in the likeness of this present world. It seems, however, that this polarity is proper to the very nature of Catholicism, while Protestantism is essentially a powerful corrective against excessive shifting of emphasis to the side of the "concrete" and visible, the ministerial and sacramental, and the human and earthly aspects.[43]

40 Leuba, J. L., *Institution und Ereignis*, 1957, 81.
41 Semmelroth, O., *Die Kirche als Ursakrament*, 1955, 81.
42 Wetter, G.P., *Charis*, 1913; Vömel, R., *Begriff der Gnade*, 1903, 39 f.
43 See "Wort und Sakrament" by Schmaus, M., in *Dogmatik* IV, 1, 25;

4. Catholic Worship

In accordance with this general outline of the Catholic character of the gospel, we may now give closer attention to a particular sphere of the Church's life: liturgical worship. It is because the Church is Catholic that her worship, like everything else, embraces the whole of her life. New Testament scholars have, however, reached completely contrary opinions in regard to this matter. At one time it was said that worship played hardly any part in the life of the early Christians; later we are told that it was the liturgical worship that determined everything. This contradiction occurred because the Catholic polarity of the gospel was not taken into account. In their worship the early Christians generally used commonplace words and expressions, but in their daily life they often used liturgical phrases. This indicates that their life, in both aspects, was centered "in Christ" for in Him both worship and life are wholly united. His own life and work took place apart from Jewish temple worship because His "holy acts" remained within the setting of natural conditions; on the other hand, however, His whole life was a perfect act of *sacrificial worship,* which is the true meaning and purpose of all religious worship. When the action of God is invisibly operative within a human deed, we call it a liturgical event. This was the mystery of the entire, visible and natural life of Jesus, and of His Passion. For this reason the Epistle to the Hebrews described His Passion in terms of "leitourgia," i.e. a representative act of sacrifice (8:6). However,

---

"analogia entis und fidei" by Söhngen, G., Einheit in der Theologie, 235 ff; "Allg. und besondere Heiligkeit" by R. Guardini, Glaubenserkenntnis, 146 ff; "Amt und Gemeinde" by Semmelroth, "Sakralität und Weltlichkeit" by Bonhoeffer, p. 64, *op. cit.*

Paul also uses this same word in referring to the Christian's life of faith and work of charity (Phil. 2:17, 30), and for Luke it seems to have been a familiar designation for any act of worship (Acts 13:12). Consequently, they could only express themselves in the consciousness that the Church lives "in Christ." (The similar, late-Jewish usage of this term had a legalistic basis that was foreign to New Testament thought.) Nevertheless, it is because the Church is not Christ Himself and is not permitted merely to imitate Him, but in all of her worship must point to the sacrificial worship of Christ which is invisibly contained in the liturgy, that its *leitourgia* must be built upon this polar duality of general and particular worship.

a) *The Worship of the Church in General*

In the sayings of Jesus we find but little mention of His sacrifice although this was of greater importance than anything else that He did. In the writings of the apostles the right understanding of His sacrifice is explained at great length while there are only brief allusions to the worship of the Church. However, this proves nothing against the importance of worship. To begin with, in the Epistle to the Romans (12:1) the whole Christian life is presented from the standpoint of sacrifice and service to God, and the whole missionary activity of the Apostle (15:16) is described as a "holy act of worship" whereby, as a priest of Christ, "the offering up of the Gentiles" may be effected. Elsewhere, the nature of the Church is defined as a "holy temple" (I Pet. 2:5) in which "spiritual sacrifices" are offered up. Finally, in II Tim. 4:6, the expression *"poured out in sacrifice"* is used almost as a synonym for martyrdom even as the word *"deliverance"* is meant to signify death. Until recently, exegesis considered these expressions as largely allegorical, but it is now increasingly admitted that we must take them seriously as a *theological statement* concerning the very nature of the Church and the apostolate.[44] Consequently, we are here confronted with a doctrinal aspect of the New Testament which has been given too little consideration in Evangelical Churches. The idea of the Body of Christ acquires its full meaning for the individual Christian primarily because of this dual aspect, for the Christian's whole life, suffering and prayer are seen under this double aspect: there is the immediate and practical behavior and, simultaneously, on the "liturgical" level it is a sacrifice before God, which completes "what is lacking of the sufferings of Christ" for the benefit of His whole mystical Body (Col. 1:24).[45] In this respect, the distinction between an expiatory sacrifice and a thank-offering apparently has no real place in the New Testament. In any case, in the Epistle to the Philippians (2:17) Paul had in mind the official temple sacrifice in which the libation was essential and which had value primarily as an expiatory sacrifice. The decisive question of the Bible is whether a sacrifice is "pleasing" to God and therefore of any value at all (Is. 56:7). The sacrifices of Christians are "spiritual sacrifices acceptable to God through Jesus Christ" (I Pet. 2:5).[46] The earlier question that was posed is now also resolved, in that love can possess expiatory efficacy, as for example I Pet. 4:8.

44 Weiss, K., *Paulus—Priester der christlichen Kultgemeinde,* in Theol. Literaturzeitung, 1954, 355 ff; and Seidensticker, Ph., *Lebendiges Opfer,* 1954.

45 Käsemann, E., *Leib und Leib Christi,* 1933, 146.

46 Bonhoeffer, *op. cit.,* 175.

b) *The Worship of the Church in Particular*

Any sacrifice offered by Christians is without value "by itself" and that is why there must always be a continual participation in the sacrifice of Christ (Heb. 4:16; 10:22; 12:22). This expression is here used in a purely ritual sense [46a] (like the Hebrew word *Corban* as the equivalent of "the Sacrifice"). In this idea of participation the Old Testament apprehends the unfathomable reality of the sacrifice. All of the ceremonies together with the offering that is sacrificed, the immolation and the burning, etc., are only the means to achieve this participation. The Epistle to the Hebrews (10:20) conceives of the mystery of Christ's sacrifice in accordance with this same idea: He passed "through the veil (that is, his flesh)" or in other words, through the surrender of His life, as our High Priest proceeding into the true and heavenly sanctuary. This same concept is also used to describe the nature of the Eucharist, the Supper of the Lord (10:19 ff.), for in their celebrations of this rite (to which the reference in this instance most certainly pertains) [47] Christians are themselves to follow "in virtue of the blood of Christ a new and living way." We are therefore *to consider the sacrifice on the Cross and the celebration of the Eucharist as a unique and conjoined happening,* by which Christians not only benefit from the fruit of the sacrifice of the Cross, but also participate in the earthly and heavenly worship of their High Priest. It is consequently almost self-evident that in the time of the apostles the Lord's Supper was al-

[46a] Schneider, in *Theologisches Wörterbuch zum Neuen Testament,* II, 682.

[47] Michel in *Theologisches Wörterbuch zum Neuen Testament,* V, 216, 16; Hahn, W., *Gottesdienst und Opfer Christi,* 1951, 111.

ready being called a "sacrifice." [48] Somewhat differently, and from a more earthly point of view, Paul said the same thing. The Lord's Supper is the "communion of the body and blood of Christ" (I Cor. 10:16), and therefore not only a communion with the person of Christ, but with the actual oblation of the Body and Blood. In Paul's conception of the liturgical celebration it is not the eating but rather the Breaking of Bread that is given the greatest emphasis, not the drinking but the blessing of the Chalice, not a passive reception but an active deed. In regard to this deed, Paul comes close to the root of the matter (I Cor. 11:26). For in this rite Christians "proclaim the death of the Lord" or more precisely they "proclaim" this death in a way that corresponds to the proclamation of a law or of a command of the emperor which only becomes authoritative through proclamation.[49] Naturally, proclamation is also preaching, and consequently the audible and sacramentally visible Word from the Cross, which the heart understands, must lead to praise and devotion. Our worship of God is therefore Christian and Catholic. For here again we find a governing principle of internal *Catholic polarity*. On the one hand there is Christ as the Word, together with God, in relation to the Church, and on the other hand as the Head of the Church in relation to God. His *leitourgia* on the Cross is one with the liturgy of the Church and with the personal self-oblation of her members as well as their liturgical celebrations. Christ did not celebrate the Lord's Supper as though He were instituting a sacrament in an arbitrary way, for He was intensely aware of the unity of His body with the temple worship of Jerusalem (Jn. 2:19) and of His sacrifice with the Pass-

48 Didache 14, Adam in *Wort und Dienst,* 1957, 111.
49 Käsemann, E., *op. cit.,* 178.

over and the feasts of His disciples. On this higher sacramental level the repetition of this rite is likewise a participation in the sacrifice of the Cross both historically and transcendently. It therefore serves as a "memorial" of Jesus, not as though there were any danger of forgetting Him without this liturgical commemoration, but rather as a remembrance of His death before God (see Lev. 2:2, 2:12; 6:8, et al) i.e. to preserve His death from the power of historical transitoriness.[50] This rite is therefore Catholic because in every particular instance it comprises in itself the one and only *leitourgia* of the whole Church, in union with Christ, including her members in heaven. Consequently, the "participation" mentioned in the Epistle to the Hebrews is also a joining in "the company of many thousands of angels and . . . the spirits of the just made perfect" (Heb. 12:22 ff.). We do not know, and can hardly now determine just how that first generation conceived of the unity of the earthly and heavenly Church whose visible appearance was soon expected, so that Paul could use an Old Testament statement concerning the angels in reference to Christians without any special explanation (Ps. 88:8; I Thess. 1:10). When however several generations of faithful members of the Church could be numbered in the ranks of the heavenly Church, particularly after their martyrdom, and an early, visible communion with the heavenly Church could no longer be expected, it became an acute question to determine the proper expression and practical manifestation which this communion should take. This question, however, was then resolved by that liturgical directive of the primitive era: "remember the sinner

[50] Jeremias, J. *Zur Exegese der Abendmahlsworte in Evangelische Theologie,* 1949, 62; Jeremias, J., on *Mark,* 14, 9 in Zeitschrift f. neutest. Wissenschaft, 1952-53, 106, vgl. Stellungnahme dazu von Öpke in Theol. Literaturzeitung, 1955, Heft 3.

before God and the Saints" (I Clement 56:1). Inevitably the saints no longer living on earth were soon included. The pagan custom of offering sacrifices to the dead over their graves in order to invoke their protection and help became an especially burning question. Was this demoniacal relationship with the dead to be opposed in a merely negative way? Was it not better to testify that within the Church there is an even closer communion between this world and the other, so that the pagan cry, "Protect us!" which was uttered over the graves of their pagan dead was changed into the Christian's invocation, "Pray for us!"? [51] There is a real danger that such an invocation might bring pagan practices into the Church, but the danger is quite as great that without it the New Testament unity of the earthly and heavenly Church could be lost completely. We are not likely to find a way out of the impasse without this clear distinction between "invocation" and "adoration."

c) *The Church's Ministry*

A sacrament requires a strictly given order. There can be no arbitrary factor whatever, for otherwise there could be no practical "apprehension" of the mystery as the concrete here and now of salvation. This is why Paul could refer to "a sacramental terminology, unmistakably recognizable, which was already in common use" and was authoritative even to himself, as an apostle, and could also allude to a common "practice." [52] Consequently, Paul insisted very emphatically on the regular observance in all places of the ordinances and traditions which he had personally given or transmitted (I Cor. 11:2, 16). One of the most important of these ordinances, designated as "jus sacrum" by Harnack [53] and as "sacred canon law" by Holl,[54] is the ministry of the Church. For unless there is a group of men in a special relationship to other men, representing Christ in relation to the Church, there can be no sacrament at all. This same distinction and contrast is found throughout the New Testament, quite apart from this particular rite. The "sacramental" acts in general are reserved to the presbyters (I Tim. 4:14),[55] (Jas. 5:14) [56] and the ministering of sacramental sacrifices to the poor is considered as part of the rite itself,[57] for which the presbyters had been set apart specifically.

The ministry, however, possesses sacramental character in itself because the invisible presence of Christ and the hidden, future nature of the Church appear in temporary form within it. It has already been said that Jesus "created" the Twelve (Mk. 3:14) in order that the Church might be "represented" in them.[58] *Whatever belongs to the Church as a whole was committed to them "in particular"—i.e. a participation in the ministry of Christ.* "It pertains to the very nature of the ministry to represent the Church in its totality, i.e. the Church comprising not only all of her members but the Head of the Church also." [59] The Apostles, and after them the presbyter-

53 Harnack, A., *Kirchenverfassung.* . . . 1910, 101.

54 Holl, K., *Gesammelte Aufsätze* II, 54.

55 Bultmann, R., *Theologie des Neuen Testaments,* 453.

56 Van d. Leeuw, G., *op. cit.,* p. 125.

57 Sohm, R., *Kirchenrecht* I, 73.

58 Bultmann, *op. cit.,* p. 60.

59 Sommerlath, E., *Amt und allgemeines Priestertum* in Schriften des Konvents Augsb. Bekenntnisses, 5, 1953, 52 f.

bishops, possessed the office of *"episkopé,"* a "title acknowledging the authority of Jesus at work within His Church." [60] The ministry of Christ is prophetical, royal and priestly, for even if Jesus Himself was not addressed as a priest but only as "Master" and "Lord" it is nevertheless His priestly office that is of greatest importance. The same is true of the Church as a whole (I Pet. 2:9) and of every individual member of the ministry also. In the New Testament, however, the presbyter-bishops are not called "priests" because if this term had been used the priestly character of the Church itself would have been blurred in the eyes of both Jews and Gentiles. The situation is wholly reversed in our time, however, for wherever the clergy are no longer accorded the title and status of priesthood it will be found that the priestly nature of the whole Christian life is no longer understood either, and consequently, an external literalism in the use of New Testament terminology can result in the complete reversal of its original meaning. In order to say that Christ, the one and only High Priest, was present in every individual member of the ministry, all of the presbyters in post-apostolic times were called "high priests." [61]

There is still another essential difference between the Christian and pagan priesthoods. Among Christians the "sacramental" office cannot be held by a woman. In Hellenism, at the time the New Testament was being written, more and more women were becoming priestesses. The Apostles strongly opposed any tendency of this kind within the Churches (see I Cor. 14:34 ff, I Tim. 2:12) although they gave open approval and encouragement to other work undertaken by women in these same

[60] Beyer in *Theologisches Wörterbuch zum Neuen Testament* II, 611.
[61] Didache 13, 1; Tertullian, *de bapt.* 17.

Churches.[62] The Church's Ministry makes visible the face to face relationship of Christ and the Church as the priestly face to face relationship of the heavenly bridegroom and His Bride (Eph. 5:23). The relationship of man and wife, face to face, corresponds to this relationship of Christ and the Church. The headship and lordship of God are both essential to the nature of Christ and to man (I Cor. 11:3; I Tim. 2:12). Wherever it is no longer customary to distinguish clearly between the ecclesiastical work that is proper to women and the sacramental offices that are reserved to men, there is a denial of the specific relation between creation and salvation, and the nature of sex and sacrament is violated. However, individual members of the Church should never be merely a flock without a shepherd, and this holds true for the clergy also. It is for this reason, according to the New Testament, that the ministry is organized as a hierarchy, a sacred ladder, as it were, in which on the one hand we find an order of *authority* demanding obedience, and on the other hand an order of brotherly companionship, necessarily interpenetrating in a manner that is never quite rationally conceivable. The distinguishing differences within the group of disciples, as between Peter, the Twelve, and the Seventy, or among those in the primitive Church—Peter, the Twelve, and the "deacons," or the gradually ascending differentiation between bishops (as the successors of the apostles and prophets), presbyters and deacons—were not mere differences in rank *(kleros,* I Pet. 5:3) [63] but different levels in essence as well. Here we find that a particular power of the Body of Christ becomes apparent, for as Luke tells us especially

[62] Käsemann, E., *Anteil der Frauander Wortverkündigung nach dem Neuen Testament.*

[63] Nauck, W., *Probleme frühchristlichen Amtsverständnisses in ZNTM,* 1955, p. 276 ff.

with regard to "the ministers of his time," [64] both Peter and John were endowed with the power of transmitting the Holy Spirit, a power which neither Simon Magus, although baptized, nor Philip the "deacon" possessed (Acts 8:14 ff).

The very difficult question of ecclesiastical government was essentially solved by Jesus Himself, for the prototype of the Church's ministry was the group of the Twelve. Within this group Peter was distinguished in a manner that is difficult to describe. We can only say that the ministry of Christ in which the Church as a whole and her clergy individually are participating, was transmitted to Peter as an individual and was an instance of unique particularity. A particular man was addressed, and yet it is truly breath-taking when we remember what was said to him. He is called the "Rock"—a term that was widely used—and is to be the very foundation of the Church (Mt. 16:18) although such an expression would properly be used only in reference to the Messias (Mt. 21:42 f). He is given the "keys of the kingdom" (Mt. 16:19) which were, however, in the keeping of Christ in heaven (Apoc. 3:7). The whole flock is entrusted to him (Jn. 21:15 ff) even though Christ is *the* Shepherd of this flock (Jn. 10:12). John tells us in significant phrases (Jn. 21:11) that he and the other disciples had caught the fish in the net (of the Church) but that Peter alone drew the net to shore without breaking it. This indicates clearly enough that this office was not intended only for the beginnings of the Church, for it did not have any part in its establishment, but was to exist for the government of the Church and as a protection against her destruction. Christ's mandate would be meaningless if it had been meant only for the

64 Campenhausen, v. H., *Kirchliches Amt*, 1953, 168.

Church of that first age. The Acts seem like a commentary
on the sayings of Jesus. The arrangement of the first part
obviously serves the purpose of proving to Christians the
great importance of this office as a truth of revelation
whose task is to guard the order and membership of the
Church. If there is less mention of this office in the second
part of Acts it does not mean that the man who, later on,
is always addressed as the "Rock" and held in high esteem,
was no longer in this position of primacy. The Acts point
even more emphatically to a later development of this
office because there was an obvious intention to indicate
a shift of the center of gravity from Jerusalem, the original
center of the Church, towards Rome, the new and growing
center, whose local church possessed such authority that
Paul could write (Rom. 16:16) "All the churches of Christ
salute you." Anyone, however, who expects to find a pre-
cise statement in the New Testament regarding the en-
durance of Peter's office is misunderstanding the very
nature of revelation as it is presented in the New Testament. It is not scientific research alone that has the right
to make judgments about this, for we must also consider
the prophecy attested by the New Testament. At this point
it may be of some importance to observe the measure of
agreement between what was expected of the Roman
church and its bishops from the very beginning and what
Peter had received from the Lord both as a mandate and
a promise. For the bishops of Rome were instrumental,
in a high degree, in keeping the gates of the Church closed
to the great movements of heresy [65] while leaving them
open to all those whom an erroneous rigorism would have
excluded. It was they who guided the Church rightly

[65] Bultmann, R., *op. cit.,* p. 482.

through the formulation of the early creeds [66] and the establishment of a new canon of faith based upon the New Testament.[67] In this activity they may also have done things that could only deserve the other saying addressed to Peter, "Get thee behind me, Satan; thou savourest not the things that be of God but those that be of men" and if this be true, the parallel is even more deserving of consideration.

At this point, primarily, an error arises when the Catholic polarity of the Church is disregarded. The polarity appears, for example, in the words that Jesus addressed to Peter: "But I have prayed for thee . . . strengthen thy brethren" (Lk. 22:32). One is the shepherd, for whom Jesus expresses the greatest concern, but he is nevertheless only a brother among brethren. "The office is not a power that is self-sufficient" [68] for while it certainly is representative of the Body of Christ, it is not however that Body apart from the complementary Church. The office and the Church are not in juxtaposition, but each of them, paradoxically, is superior to the other. The apostles never cease to lay emphasis upon freedom, independence and immediate access to God, commending and fostering them in the Church while also stressing the importance of general unity both in work and in doctrine (I Jn. 2:27; II Cor. 1:24; Rom. 15:14). This is true in regard to the relationship between all of the clergy and the Church, and also the relationship between the chief pastoral office and the other organs and members of the Church.

Obviously, if the ministry itself is "sacramental" then its transmission, also, is a sacramental act. But what is the

[66] Kattenbusch, F., *Das apostolische Symbol,* II, 1900, 712.

[67] Harnack, A., *Dogmengeschichte,* I, 481 ff and 485; also: Harnack, A., *Die Entstehung des Neuen Testaments,* 1914, 76.

[68] Campenhausen, H., *op. cit.,* p. 327.

sign required for it? Shall we agree with the historic
Church that requires ordination derived by direct transmission from the apostles? We cannot expect to find a
direct answer to this question in the New Testament because the latter was written at a time when the apostles
were still living. But we should give consideration to two
significant points: the apostles took over the Jewish custom
of the laying-on of hands which was meant to signify the
unity of anyone ordained in this manner with the one
whom God had sent (Moses) (Mt. 23:2).[69] This was in line
with the fact that the disciples and envoys of the apostles
were given an authority similar to that of the apostles
themselves (II Cor. 7:15; Tit. 2:15) which was not to end
with their lives but was to be transmitted to others.
Furthermore, the New Testament, in contrast to Judaism,
considers the transmission of the ministry to be an immediate working of the Spirit (Apoc. 20:28) and a direct
gift of the Risen One (Eph. 4:11). This prevents us from
considering the transmission of the ministry in too me-
chanical a manner. However, with our present knowledge
of the New Testament revealing that all offices are com-
prised within the *one* office, the one "leitourgia" of the
Church, now accorded such importance, we will be able
to deal with the question concerning ordination and determine whether the relationship between the primitive
Church and the apostles can be found in a form intended
by the Holy Spirit and sacramentally required.

d) *Ecclesiastical Tradition*

The last mentioned question is one of many which the

69 Lohse, Ed., *Ordination im Spätjudentum und im Neuen Testament,*
1951, 53 ff.

New Testament clearly considers of vital importance in the very life of the Church, but does not provide any answer. The "good doctrine" however cannot simply be found in the New Testament. Questions concerning the relationship between Word and Sacrament, charisma and office, or regarding confession as required according to John 20:23, or the nature of "leitourgia"—are all of them questions arising out of necessity, but none of these questions are answered for us. In short, "the third article is still incomplete." [70] The New Testament alludes to forms required for celebration of the sacraments, called "traditions" which we are unable to know more exactly, but which require further development. The Church has had the courage to make decisions in such matters and consequently has made uniformity of doctrine and sacramental acts really possible. In doing this the Church has followed the example of the New Testament itself.

It was, of course, quite astonishing that Jesus Himself never wrote down any of His sayings. He wanted His Word to come into the world as the Word of Salvation, through the very thought and experience of the *Church*. *Thus, the Word of the New Testament originated from the start as "tradition" to be faithfully held, while transforming the gift according to the situation.* This "tradition" is an essential part of the mystery of the rite, i.e. the presence of Christ, and of His Word and His Work. In conjunction with this there is also His presence in the sacrament which requires the external tradition, the authoritative arrangement of the office and of the forms of the rite. *In this tradition, however, God has provided an indispensable connection of the apostolic era with all later times.* The first period is the time of the birth of the

70 Conzelmann, H., *Mitte der Zeit,* 1954, 197.

Church [71] when God, acting through the apostles and the primitive Church, created the true form for the Word of His Son in the writings of the New Testament, and also created the fundamental structure of the ministry and the liturgy.[72] This connection of the original era and a later time, as of scripture and tradition, actually represents the relationship existing between Christ and His Church.

Over and over again the Church has overcome the danger that this connection is no longer authentic. Holy Scripture gradually came to be regarded as hardly more than material for verifying the thought structure of ecclesiastical doctrine. The importance of tradition and of logical deduction increasingly replaced the experience of ever-renewed listening to the voice of the Good Shepherd in the Scriptures. The Reformation was a powerful reaction which aimed to restore the full importance of Holy Scripture, but how can we explain that even the Scriptures, as shown earlier, were given only a one-sided validity even in the Reformed Churches also, although largely unintentionally? Is it perhaps because tradition is considered to be merely "human custom" as compared with God's Word in the Scriptures? But this would be a contradiction of the Scriptures which, in addition to the parting words of the apostles, also include the forward-looking words of the prophets (of the New Testament!) (Eph. 2:20, 4:11), but even our own understanding of the Scriptures was absolutely juxtaposed to all preceding "tradition," although it can never be anything else but tradition, namely a faithful transmission of the Word suitable according to a particular situation. *The fullness of Holy Scripture can*

[71] Rahner, K., *Über die Schriftinspiration* in Zeitschrift f. kath. Theologie, 1956, 137 ff.

[72] Lietzmann, H., *Messe und Herrenmahl*, 1926, 181.

only enter into the thought and life and form of the Church when the fullness of tradition is also taken seriously in its divinely determined relation to Holy Scripture, in spite of all the possible and actual errors in its development. Certainly there is danger in this polarity of scripture and tradition, but if we try to avoid it by overemphasizing one of the two components in our transmission of Christian truth, we may lose what should have been preserved: the authority of the divine Word, the voice of the ever-present Lord.

RICHARD BAUMANN

CATHOLIC TRUTH IN THE NEW TESTAMENT

II. ORDER AND AUTHORITY IN THE CHURCH

Order and authority are already revealed in the very first verse of the New Testament. "The book of the origin of Jesus Christ, the Son of David, the son of Abraham." The origin of Jesus points back to the origin of Adam, to God's creation of the world. There are two orders of the one and only God: the order of creation in which all men exist, and the order of grace, fully revealed to us in the Son of God who is also the Son of Man. Order is the work of God. It is not added to life as though it were something external or arbitrary. In itself it is the life of God embracing us. We have the true life only as long as we are living within God's order and have His order within ourselves. We experience the miracle of the order of salvation as soon as we acknowledge the authority of Jesus. Even the very last verse of the Bible speaks of the authority of the One over all: "The grace of our Lord Jesus Christ be with all."

Although the Son of God is unique, it was nevertheless as man that He entered into the already existing order of authority of the chosen people of God. The Anointed

One, the Messias, the future king of salvation, took His place in the succession of David the king and prophet, and of the patriarch Abraham, together with the whole line of generations of those who had been appointed by the Covenant to guide God's own people. God had sent His servants, and finally His Son, and now the Son would send forth servants, brethren and friends until the end of time. In His threefold office as king, priest and prophet, Jesus unites within Himself all authority of kings, priests and prophets. He appeared, publicly associating Himself with John the Baptist, literally repeating the latter's message: "Repent ye: for the kingdom of heaven is at hand." The people thought of Him as a prophet. But He was more than that, for it was from Bethlehem that should come forth "a leader who shall rule my people Israel" (Mt. 2:6), literally meaning "who will lead my people to the pasture." As the Messias of Israel, Jesus had also to gather unto God all the Gentile nations in order that there might be one flock under one shepherd. Jesus accomplished this great deed through obedience to His Father, even unto death upon the Cross, by sacrificing Himself as the One in atonement for the sins of all men. The Lamb of God with His sacrifice of reconciliation is therefore the Priest who offers sacrifice, mediates, prays and blesses. He is the Prophet and the King, and is also become a high priest forever "according to the order of Melchisedech" (Heb. 6:20). Jesus died in fulfillment of His authority. His Father has authenticated this by the Resurrection, the Ascension, and the sending forth of the Holy Spirit.

How does Jesus who, as the king, sits at the right hand of the Father and as the heavenly High Priest, the prophet of an eternal gospel, enable people of all generations to participate in salvation? Jesus is our Emmanuel, for in

Him "God-with-us" has appeared among us. Born of a
woman, He became man, taking our humanity up into
the covenant of God, and therefore He allows man to participate in His work for all time, in order that the image
of God, reconstituted and renewed in men, might glorify
God. "All power in heaven and on earth is given me,"
Jesus says to the disciples as they wait to receive their mission from Him. "Go, therefore, and make disciples of all
nations, baptizing them in the name of the Father, and of
the Son, and of the Holy Spirit, teaching them to observe
all that I have commanded you." This is a common work
embracing all future generations. His work and ours! "I
am with you all days, even unto the consummation of the
world."

The authority vested in us by Jesus was given in order
to allow His authority its fullest power; the work of salvation, completed by Himself, can thus bear fruit in space
and time. This authority is royal, priestly and prophetic,
for it is His own. "You, however, are a chosen race, a
royal priesthood, a holy nation, a purchased people; that
you may proclaim the perfections of him who has called
you out of darkness into his marvelous light" (I Pet. 2:9).
"*You*" means the whole Church, with every individual
Christian participating in the mission. Affirming and realizing what he has become by the grace of God, the Christian, as free as a king, can then be his brother's shepherd
and keeper in charity. In a priestly manner he stands before God, summoned by the Lamb of God to share in the
sacrifice of His own life to the Father. As a mediator he
prays for us, helping others to overcome their faults and
failings, and gives his blessing. He cannot do otherwise,
for he must proclaim the salvation he has experienced,
telling the world both by the word and by his wordless

behavior. The threefold authority of the individual Christian is present only within the Body of Christ. All Christians are members of His Body; but not all are of the same rank, nor do they all have the same activity (I Cor. 12). Jesus completed the Old Testament, His Father's work. The people of the Covenant were not a mere multitude but were organized as a nation whose order was established by God. The organization of the Covenant allowed for a hierarchy of graduated authority: Moses and Aaron and the Seventy, heads of tribes and families, the orders of the holy servants, each with its own function, and kings, priests and prophets. All of this was fulfilled and comprehended in the "Consummatum est" of the Savior. But the nation of the New Covenant, as the body of Christ, was to be even more perfectly organized. In the order of this body there are those who are sent, and first among them was Peter. Next there were the Seventy, being prophets, preachers of the gospel, shepherds and teachers (Eph. 4); and then the bishops, presbyters and deacons (Pastoral Epistles), together with those who possessed various charismata accorded to some for the exorcism of demons, and for healing, prophesy and the working of miracles (Mt. 10; Rom. 12; I Cor. 12). It is the Son of God who, in His Testament, willed the basic form for the order of all authority during the whole time of salvation. The Holy Spirit recalls the words of this Testament to our minds over and over again, and develops them in a process of divine-living growth. The omnipotence of the Father maintains the work accomplished by the Son, for what God has created He also preserves.

It is the servants of the Word who proclaim as truth and reality whatever has originated in Christ. They obey the Word and consequently they are His witnesses, even in

the face of judgment and unto their death as martyrs. For
they know that the Lord watches over His holy order.
Christ protects those whom He has sent and their message
also. The authority of the organs of the covenant is an
authority originating in Him, the creator and lord of all
authority, the sovereign judge. He is vigilant in guarding
the legitimate order from generation to generation. He
punishes the breaking of the law and any illegal act. Anyone who defies the authority of those whom Christ has
sent, has defied Christ Himself, for His authority remains
forever.

Christians are united in their affirmation of the threefold office of Jesus Christ. Lutherans fundamentally acknowledge the continuation of the derived threefold
function of the Church, individual Christians, and all
public organs established by the covenant, in accordance
with the testament of Jesus. But where then did the schism
occur?

We are proud of the freedom of the universal priesthood and of our free access to the Scriptures. "Whoever
is proud, shall be proud of the Lord" and, as a free member of the community should claim this authority in taking his stand before God in the manner of a priest. For
when we are witnessing for Christ we are interpreting the
Scriptures. However, even in Jesus' time the sacred writings were not self-explanatory. In the synagogue at Ca-
pharnaum, Jesus reached for the Book, read from it and
then explained the passage. The Sermon on the Mount
abounds in scriptural interpretations, but Jesus explained
them all in *His* own way, in contrast to the opinions of
the elders. Teachers of great renown gave their particular
explanations, as did the Scribes and the Pharisees. The
Scriptures were always the same, and yet Jesus explained

them in such a way that He was condemned to death. Even the Risen Christ continued revelation by expounding the Scriptures. "And beginning then with Moses and with all the Prophets, he interpreted to them in all the Scriptures the things referring to himself" (Lk. 24:27). His disciples followed His example. It was Peter's confession of faith at Caesarea Philippi which contained the decisive interpretation of all Scripture, acknowledging Jesus as the Messias whom the Scriptures had promised and foretold. And immediately the Lord appointed Peter to be the authoritative interpreter, teacher and leader of God's own people because he had received this revelation from God Himself. In Matthew 16:19 the expression *bind and loose* means to function with authority in doctrinal and disciplinary decisions for the Church. Peter's proclamation at Pentecost (Acts 2:14-41), contains from the very beginning a fully authoritative interpretation of scripture, a doctrinal decision and a disciplinary decree concerning members of the "House of Israel." However, the other apostles, the preachers of the gospel and the prophets of revelation, were also authorized to interpret scripture and to teach, and even make judicial decrees as executors of the Will of God (Mt. 18:18). But there was one thing they never did. They did not lay the Bible on the table "to explain itself." If you are a Protestant Christian, is there anyone who interprets the Bible for you when you read it? Or does it explain itself? Are you able to interpret the Scriptures yourself? Or is the Holy Spirit doing this for you? However, you do not interpret the Bible in the manner of the Jews, nor has it the same meaning for you as for atheists and apostates who "leave the Bible" to the Hebrews of ancient times because they can no longer make head or tail of it.

We approach the Bible as baptized Christians, following from the first the interpretations of the Christian Church which is led by the Holy Spirit into all truth. On the other hand, we begin our reading as members of one of the denominations of Protestantism whose founders and leaders have influenced our thinking, even subconsciously, generally from early childhood, long before our reading has ever begun. The translation we are using has itself been influenced by the translators. And who are they? What earlier interpreters did they follow? Were they members of the community which constituted the authoritative order of the Church of the New Covenant, established by the Lord Himself, which was formed on the first Pentecost, and of which the Holy Spirit keeps all generations mindful forever? "Knowing of whom thou hast learned," wrote Paul to his disciple, Timothy, and because "from thy infancy thou hast known the Sacred Writings," the apostle admonishes him to follow the teaching of those who had expectantly awaited the Messias, and then the doctrine of the Lord and of His Apostles, including both the original Twelve and also Paul who was called last. As a bishop, Timothy adhered to this doctrinal tradition and subsequently he required the pastors of the local churches to follow it. The very content of the epistles to Timothy and Titus proves that there is, according to God's order, a succession of authorized interpreters and teachers of scripture within the Church of the Holy Spirit. No one can ever claim possession of authority to interpret the Scriptures contrary to the teaching of those to whom Christ has publicly given this authority. But the Christian who knows the teacher from whom the doctrine was received, may himself now earnestly search the Scriptures, and inspired by the Holy Spirit, poured out upon all who are within the Body of Christ, can possess power to discover new treasures and become a witness whose testimony will have real force. If you possess a prophetic gift, it must be in accordance with the faith of the Church of God. Even the most powerful testimony, required by the Lord and addressed to the appointed teachers, does not annul the existing order of authority but should even strengthen it. First the Apostles, and after them the prophets: this was the established rank and order. Those who receive special gifts and charismata have their rightful place within the Church through the one Spirit of Truth, and for the benefit of all members, in the service of charity. But the pastors must even watch over the most gifted, according to the exhortation of the apostle: "Take heed to yourselves and to the whole flock in which the Holy Spirit has placed you as bishops, to rule the Church of God, which he has purchased with his own blood" because "from your own selves men will rise speaking perverse things, to draw away the disciples after them" (Acts 20). But who will determine this perversity? The false teachers and founders of sects were always certain that they alone were proclaiming the truth in which the Scriptures were interpreted to them by the Holy Spirit Himself. This accounts for their behavior and the number of their followers. They looked upon all other Christians as perverse. However, that they were "speaking perverse things" was the belief of the apostle Paul who, from the beginning, was in full agreement with the original Twelve. It was also the judgment of all the bishops and presbyters of the early Church in their unity of faith. Those who possessed real authority were involved by the rebels in a life and death struggle for the sheep of the flock. An example is seen in Paul's condemnations of the seducer of the Galatians (Gal. 1:9). "If anyone preach a gospel to you other than that which you have received, let him be anathema!"

If every baptized Christian is accorded his proper place within the order of the Church, subordinate to those who possess authority, what is the place of Evangelical pastors in the Church of the New Testament? We have "pastors" in the Lutheran Church; other denominations have their "preachers," and both terms have a meaningful relationship to the offices of Jesus as a shepherd (*pastor* is the Latin word for shepherd), and as a teacher, as also to the universal Church and its faithful members as shepherds and teachers. But what shall be said about the ordained priesthood of our Church if the whole people of the New Covenant already constitute a priesthood? The answer to this question depends on whether Evangelical Christians really have an altar on which the sacrifice of the New Covenant is offered. Our hymns strongly testify to our sharing the sacrifice with Christ as the reconciled community. And just as the Word of God uttered but once in Jesus' preaching is certainly not depreciated by our many sermons at divers times and places, but rather attains to its fullest effect and scope, the same may also be said concerning the one sacrifice of the High Priest, once offered and all-sufficient, which is offered in heaven (Apoc.) even as the Church here on earth participates in the same oblation, offering it to the Father while also offering itself, the Body of Christ of which Christ Himself is the Head. It is therefore complete in its fullness as the sacrifice of the Head with the Body, of the Messias and His people, a sacrifice of the whole Christ. However, the public liturgy, as the offering of the sacrifice for the people and with them, requires an ordained priesthood. If there really are no priests in this sense, then there are no authorized pastors or preachers either. For it is in the Lord Himself that the threefold office originated. The apostle Paul clearly understood that his vocation as a preacher was connected with his priestly office. It was "because of the grace that has been given me by God, that I should be a minister of Christ Jesus to the Gentiles; sanctifying the gospel of God, that the offering up of the Gentiles may become acceptable, being sanctified by the Holy Spirit" (Rom. 15:15). But to minister sacerdotally, "to do a priest's work" among the people, is not merely the task of a commissioned individual. If we search the Scriptures anew we will find both explicit and implicit testimony in regard to sacrifice and liturgy and the work of a priest (Phil. 2:17; Rom. 12:1). It is wholly a mystery of faith that the servant of Jesus can say, with the apostle Paul, "what is lacking of the sufferings of Christ I fill up in my flesh for his body, which is the Church; whose minister I have become in virtue of the office that God has given me in your regard. For I am to fulfill the word of God. . ." (Col. 1:24). Does the priest have no part in the one sacrifice and the mediatorship of our Lord? We must keep ever in mind that the whole Christ consists of both Head and members in unity. Together with all who are saved the minister of Jesus received the fruit of the sacrifice of atonement, given by the one Priest and Mediator. Now he must do two things: as a member of the body of Christ he enters into the sacrifice of Christ in obedience to the Head, and then, appointed by our Lord to the public office of a priest, he transmits the fruit of the sacrifice to the Christian community and through himself he makes salvation available to all men.

No man, however, takes this honor unto himself; he must first be called by God. The apostles, whose vocation was immediately from our Lord, have transmitted the commissioning from generation to generation through the laying-on-of-hands and prayer. Wherever the pastors of our Church have been ordained and invested, we have a line of succession in the office which extends back through many generations. The authoritative directive to Titus, as a bishop, is significant in this matter: "set right anything that is defective and . . . appoint presbyters in every city, as I myself directed thee to do" (Titus 1:5), which indicates the order of the early Church that included presbyters or priests, and pastors and preachers of the local churches, ordained and sent by the bishop. Our own registers of pastors bearing the names of successors in the office down through the centuries prove that we also adhere to the concept of legitimate transmission, as ordered by our Lord, by the laying-on-of-hands and prayer. It is true, however, that most of our records only carry us back to Reformation times, and we may well ask whether there should not be something to connect us with the early Church.

What may be said concerning the office of the bishop from the beginning of the Church's life? "This saying is true: If anyone is eager for the office of bishop, he desires a good work" (I Tim. 3:1). This word of the apostle Paul to Timothy, the bishop, is read in our churches together with other sayings concerning the ministry. If the testimony of the New Testament in regard to bishops is the Word of God, then the office of the bishop has certainly not been lost at any time. The apostles themselves were pastors and bishops as the heads of their communities. Consequently, it is by God's authority and will that the office of the bishop exists from the very beginnings of the New Covenant down through all the centuries since. The Holy Spirit has kept us mindful of this through all succeeding generations. "As for you, let that which you have heard from the beginning abide in you. If that abides in you which you have heard from the beginning, you also will abide in the Son and in the Father" (I Jn. 2:24). The bishops participate in the threefold office of Jesus in an outstanding way, by continuing His work as pastors and heads of the churches. It is through their ministry that Christ Himself is present with His people until the end of time. They are the gift of the Risen Christ, and are the very ligaments and joints of the Body of Christ, holding together all the organs by which the whole life of all the members abides in divine growth and service.

In the Augsburg Confession of 1530, our fathers acknowledged the permanence of the episcopal office. They wanted to defend the Word of God, however, against age-long secularization and confusion of the office with earthly sovereignty by upholding the Word of God as the only guide and standard of that office. It was never their intention to interrupt the historic succession which had continued unbroken from the time of the apostles themselves. On the contrary, they were seeking an even greater apostolicity and spirituality for the episcopal office. Christ had sent forth the apostles with the command: "As the Father has sent me, I also send you. . . . Receive the Holy Spirit" (Jn. 20:22). The office of the bishop is therefore based upon divine right—*jurisdictio jure divino*—to preach the gospel, to remit sins, to make doctrinal decisions and to reject anything that contradicts the gospel, to exclude from the Church the godless whose evil works are apparent, not by human force but by the Word of God alone. Pastors and churches must consequently be obedient to the bishops, according as Christ has said (Lk. 10:16): "He who hears you, hears me. . . ." (C.A. 28). According to the belief of the Augsburg Fathers, ordination and commissioning by word, prayer and the sacrament of the laying-on-of-hands are also essential for succession in the office of a bishop. They were "strongly in favor of preserving the old canonical order and government by bishops" (Apology XIV, also see Article X, Schmalkalden). However, it was certainly not prophetic testimony concerning the reformation of the episcopal office which was preserved, but instead, various individuals made themselves superior to it, exercising their own judgment upon the office, and finally allowed it merely functional purposes "for the sake of charity and unity, but not out of necessity." This was similar to the famous addition to the Schmalkaldian Articles by Melanchthon in which he left to the pope a governing primacy according to "human right." Those who alone had possessed authority before this time had no part in the decision concerning the content of the proclamation.

The following four centuries of struggle with the Word of God have been advantageous to all of us. From the Protestant side, the opinion of church members and of many pastors has been steadily increasing that we need bishops according to the Word of God and within the community of the one Church of Jesus Christ. However, if we admit that the Church has existed in unbroken continuity from the beginning, then it must also be acknowledged that our Lord has never abandoned it. Through the Holy Spirit the order authorized by our Lord has always been maintained. If it be said that the Church as a whole had perished, together with the community of those who derived their authority from Jesus, how would a new Church be formed? An anti-hierarchy would certainly serve no good purpose, and nothing can be really accomplished by the easy compromise of cold co-existence, which would simply recognize that there are Catholic bishops and there are Protestant bishops, each group possessing their particular authority. From the first days of the one, holy, Catholic and Apostolic Church, the term *bishop* has been used in reference to a clearly defined office, and if we were to use the same term with a different meaning it would certainly be misleading.

There is widespread uniformity of opinion concerning the real nature of episcopacy, as the passages from the Augsburg Confession clearly prove. (Many more could be cited in addition to the passages already mentioned.) The uniformity would be complete if our Protestant Churches would no longer interpret one of the *basic* doctrines of the gospel in a way that differs radically from the interpretation of the Catholic Church down through all the ages: we mean all the chapters in the New Testament which pertain to the office of Peter. In this respect the contrast is not merely affirmative and negative, but rather signifies *to be or not to be*. A successor of Peter *does exist* or else he *does not exist* in the Word of God. Expressed even more forcefully, the papacy was founded by the *Son of God* or it was founded by the *devil*. In this matter the devil and Christ confront each other. In similar vein there is contrast in the proclamation of the gospel concerning leadership in regard to universal order and authority in the Church.

Among all baptized Christians where does the real dividing line now lie? Is it between the Catholic and Eastern Orthodox bishops on the one hand, and Protestantism on the other? The Catholic Church recognizes the Orthodox bishops because they have continued in the unbroken apostolical succession by the sign of the Word and by ordination through the laying-on-of-hands and prayer.

This fact made for a greater constancy in essential doctrine. Or should the Orthodox and the Protestants be grouped together on one side, with the Catholic bishops and Peter's successor on the other? This latter grouping is more realistic in our time because of the point of view commonly taken in regard to the gospel passages where Peter is mentioned. Consequently, as far as the "Chair of Peter" is concerned, it may be said that there are two opposing pulpits in Christendom. In the one pulpit it is said that the "rock" exists as the foundation of the Church, and in Peter's successors will be found the shepherd of the flock, the keeper of the keys and the first among all teachers according to the gospel. In the other pulpit we are told that such an office does not exist. The same gospel is read at both altars, but contradictory interpretations and proclamations are preached in the two pulpits. Obviously, one of the two preachers must be contrary to Christ in this matter, for he is preaching a different gospel.

Fortunately there is a possibility that we may be able to bridge this chasm. Scripture studies among Protestants, especially during the last fifty years, have given us new assurance that the *one* flock with the *one* shepherd of the Lord has existed continuously since the Ascension and Pentecost, not only because of unity in baptism and faith, the breaking of bread and prayer, but primarily as a union of Christians under a recognized authority, with Peter, the *rock,* as the one shepherd representing the one Christ. We began to realize that the order of authority, in the beginning, did have a head, and not merely for human reasons but in accordance with Christ's command. It was therefore based upon both divine and human right. We now admit that the constitution of the early Church included the primacy, and to this extent the chasm has been bridged. However, was not this order intended only for the Church in its origins? Or was it meant to be permanent? The word of the Lord concerning the organization of the Church is everlasting, as a part of the gospel itself, and the glad tidings were meant for us also. Surely it is the prerogative of Christ to govern His Church in the way that was revealed in the beginning, and this must be a prerogative which He still preserves and exercises. Does the Last Will of Christ make reference to the pastoral office of the *one?* Is it not an integral part of His Testament? Quite recently the objection has been made that "there is no passage in the New Testament which suggests the idea that he (Peter) had been told to transfer his primacy among the apostles to certain successors" (*Christian Religion,* by O. Simmel, S.J. and R. Stählin, Frankfurt, 1957, page 22, Evangelical Contribution). But is this a tenable opinion? The same objection could properly be made against the continuation of all other commissions made by Our Lord as well. All of them were directed to individuals at a particular time and place in specific terms. An attempt could perhaps be made to except the pastoral office of the *one,* but in Jesus' own words, "He that hears you, heareth me" also included the one apostle who was the first and the leader.

We should determine whether Jesus' sayings to the apostles generally were meant to include Peter also, and we will find that they did. Since we cannot omit him from the indivisible, living order of the community addressed by Jesus, we would find it necessary to confine the integral mission of the Church and finally the whole gospel itself to those distant days. The Son of God, however, in addressing the men of His time, was also addressing all generations until the end of the world.

Until now, not even the office of Peter which he personally exercised in the early Church has been given any attention or emphasis in our churches, perhaps because of the imperishable duration of Jesus' own works and words. But let us face the facts, Evangelical Christian! What outstanding activity can be attributed to Peter, the "Rock," when we consider him in relation to all the apostles? Already in Acts 1, he is cited in the *first* place, and all are united with him "with one accord." He ordered the selection of another bearer of authority to take the place of the one who had fallen away: "His ministry let another take." The order of authority was then fully restored, a process accomplished within the Church. When Pentecost had come, the messengers of the gospel, in corporate unity, went forth to preach to the people of Israel, and even to the world of the Gentiles. The "Rock" appeared together with the Eleven, and preached the sermon of Pentecost. Because of the authority vested in him by our Lord he judged and interpreted the miracle of tongues, not as something fantastic but as a spiritual occurrence in fulfillment of the word of the prophet. And then he spoke of Christ and interpreted the Scriptures with authority, addressing all of the people present and the whole world as well. None of the other apostles contradicted his decision concerning the doctrine; it will continue to be binding until the end of the world. All of them followed his decision in their own teaching, freely united with him, and filled with the Holy Spirit themselves. He who was the *first* among them, and the others along with him, answered the people who were asking what was necessary for salvation.

It was Peter, and those who accompanied him, who opened the gates of the Church by holy baptism (Acts 2).

In regard to the whole body of Jewish doctrine he again made an infallible and irrevocable decision concerning the interpretation of the Scriptures with reference to the Messias, and how this should be applied to Jesus (Acts 3). Together with John he defended the Church, its authority and its message, addressing those who had formerly exercised authority over the Jews. "Neither is there salvation in any other." It was from Jesus as the Christ that the disciples had derived all "power," and for some of them even the power to work miracles (Acts 4). Within the Church, discipline was the representative of God, according to Peter (Acts 5). He was the vigilant guardian of faith for the whole Church, and when he was taken to prison he openly proclaimed the new authority as opposed to the old order until not one stone remained upon another. "We must obey God rather than men." This meant that the old rock beneath the Holy of Holies of the temple was now replaced by another *rock* in a new temple, the Church, the house of God. Peter accused the Jewish leaders of exercising a merely human authority that was now even contrary to God (Acts 5).

Peter was among all the apostles, as their leader, when the seven deacons were appointed to take care of alms and gifts (Acts 6). The men who were chosen then received the Holy Spirit through the laying-on-of-hands by Peter and other apostles. It was, however, Peter alone who exercised the power of the keys against Simon the sorcerer, guilty of "simony," the act of buying or selling ecclesiastical preferment (Acts 8). In his travels through various countries he was exercising what would now be called the visitation of the churches (Acts 9). Finally, and again acting alone, in the presence of other disciples, and as their leader, he made the most important and far-reaching decision of the early

Church, in obedience to the command of the Lord and of the Holy Spirit, opening the gates to all the Gentile nations by baptizing the first Gentile, Cornelius (Acts 10). The work of Jesus, fulfilled on the Cross, of making one creation out of two, became historical for the first time through this act of Peter. It became the work of Head and members and could only be accomplished after fierce struggles within the original Church whose first members had all been Jews. Paul, in a most forceful manner, made Peter's decision widely known, as the correct interpretation of the Lord's words concerning the Gentiles. He also became the most powerful supporter of the apostle Peter when the latter appeared to become weak in his office (Gal. chapter 2). The Keeper of the Keys based his decision upon the guidance given him by the Lord Himself, and this was also verified by the facts, which Peter explained to the Church. "On hearing this, they held their peace, and glorified God" (Acts 11). The whole order of authority, with the council of the apostles also, were in agreement with the decision made by him who was *first* among them. The unity between James, the apostle of the Jews, and Paul, the apostle of the Gentiles, would now continue, and this ensured the unity of the whole Church.

The *rock* experienced the power of his Lord and served as the foundation of the one structure, but Herod tried to overturn the whole new structure by destroying the "rock," intending to bring him to trial. But the Church, with one accord, prayed for him. God freed him, and "he departed, and went to another place" (Acts 12:17), as Jesus had instructed the persecuted to do (Mt. 10:23). However, he first ordered the Christians to give James a report. James is called the first bishop of Jerusalem, but does this mean that Simon, in that night of obedience and testimony, had

renounced his new name, and his office also, in favor of
James? Or did the Lord withdraw the office from His witness whom He had just saved and delivered in such a
miraculous way? Certainly not! For the Lord is faithful,
and the "rock," in the office given him by the Lord, glorified God in death (John 21).

We have considered the beginnings of the Church's history and her entrance into the world since Pentecost. Her
organization is clearly apparent. It was the founder of the
Church Who appointed a head for the order of authority,
just as every family or city or kingdom must have one for
leadership and preservation, and as God Himself had led
and guided the people of the Old Covenant through their
kings. But it was the Holy Spirit who recalled to our
minds certain sayings of Jesus, and more especially those
that pertained to Peter. In this respect it is particularly
significant that the Lord had given a new name to one
apostle: Peter—the *Rock*. But this was not the kind of
name that is given at birth, nor does it indicate a certain
nature (as, for instance, Sons of Thunder). *"Rock"* expresses a definite, pertinent and most important idea for
the Spirit-guided order of the Church, the very foundation of God's own people. This was also true in the history
of the Old Covenant in regard to the meaningful names
of those times: Abram, Sarai, Jacob, who became known
as Abraham, Sarah, and Israel. In each instance the individual was given an office or mission. Thereafter he has a
definite status, receives something special, and must accomplish something that is clearly specified, always in relation to the whole of God's people and nation. Now, God
is the rock and Christ is the rock. What then is the relation
of Peter to the Son of God who became man? He can be
"the rock" only in a representative manner, in the succes-

sion of Jesus, like the status of parents who are "representatives of God" in relation to their children, and as the apostles, disciples, and all other Christians are sent forth as messengers of salvation, "representing Christ" in the following of Jesus, and finally as the Church represents Him in the world. In this sense, there must be *one* to represent the Christ in His relation to the whole divine structure of the Church on earth. The functions of both the *one* and the community are closely inter-related, as the one existing for the many and the many for the one. This enables the many living stones to be *one* unity, one structure.

If this be true for every house on earth so long as the world exists, then it is also true for the Temple. Jesus used the example of the Temple in Jerusalem. This is evident because the "gates of hell" are mentioned, for according to Jewish doctrine, the sacred rock under the Holy of Holies in the Temple was the only closing stone of the gates to Sheol, the underworld of the dead. "Behold I will lay a stone in the foundations of Sion. . . ." says the prophet Isaias (28:16), in foreseeing the Messias as the future stronghold of all the faithful and as a protection against the siege of all those who have made their covenant with hell. This stone or rock of all who are within the community of faith is the man Jesus. But Jesus said, "And I also tell you: you are the rock. . . ," revealing that in His succession there must be *one* to be the God-given support and protection for all, in the concentration of strength against the overwhelming forces of falsehood, death and hell. Jesus' promise that the gates of hell would not prevail was addressed to Peter, the "rock," in very exact and specific wording. It was Peter whom the Lord was addressing in all three sayings, beginning with Mt. 16:13-18. As the "closing stone" of the portals to Sheol, it is Peter who is *first* exposed in the fiercest and most enduring manner to the attacks from below. If Peter failed, the whole of God's structure would crumble. But Peter will be upheld by the power of God and consequently the whole structure will be safe.

The *one* is the support of the many. He receives and *possesses* something from the Lord forever and ever, the "keys of the kingdom of heaven." This kingdom of heaven, or of God, during the time of salvation, is exemplified as the palace of David in the Sion that is to come. As with any other house also, it is the owner who keeps the keys: God and His Christ, the son of David. But now Jesus proclaims that He is going to hand over these symbols of His ministry and authority to one of His disciples, in fulfillment of the prophecy of Isaias (chap. 22). This passage tells of a servant to whom the king commits his own authority by giving him the keys, making the man the most powerful person both in the palace and in the kingdom itself, ranking immediately after the king, and holding the first place during the king's absence. This office, according to the prophet's account, was handed down from one holder to another. And shortly before Jesus' ascension, He put His own authority into the care and keeping of a man by transmission of the "keys." It is the keeper of the keys who has authority to decide, in the highest degree, concerning admission to the kingdom of God and the Church of Jesus Christ. He possesses the power to administer the blessings of salvation and to distribute them in accordance with the command of the Lord.

There is another kind of authority which the *one* has received and possesses, but this is shared with the others in the ministry also: the authority to "bind and loose." Nevertheless, the *one* has precedence in this instance too

(Mt. 16:19 and 18:18). The parable of "binding and loosing" originated in the language of the court as an ordinance of the Old Covenant concerning authorities where it signified "adjudging excommunication and annulling it." This also pertained to previous legal decrees or to decisions regarding doctrine. But here again Jesus did not abolish the law but fulfilled it, for in the New Covenant also it still refers to the making of doctrinal decisions based upon the Scriptures, and the condemnation of any false doctrine, with binding effect upon "teachers" of lesser rank. Matthew 16 indicates that the *one* took precedence, through God's own intervention and purpose, in revealing the everlasting and orthodox doctrine. Others can never proclaim revealed doctrine contrary to his definition, but only in union with him, no matter how God may give it to them. This is the status and relationship of the *one*, commanded by God and established in history. It is only in this matter that doctrine comes forth from one mouth, and as from one mouth only. It is therefore a matter of spiritual government, with the one and the many exercising the authority to spiritually guide and govern all the faithful in the representation of Christ and of God. Christ Jesus is the "prophet" who reveals the Father, the one and only Teacher and Master, legislator and judge. But the real effect of Jesus' mission on earth will now be accomplished through the work of the *one* together with the others. As our heavenly Lord, and yet ever present with His own, He will give power to the servants of His Will to bind and to loose in His Name. They must *do* this in obedience to Christ, and He will *confirm* what they do.

The Church therefore lives her life in *one* truth. Before His departure, in the Cenacle, the Lord again exemplified the life of the Church in the relationship of the "one for the many" (Lk. 22:31-32). It is the adversary who began the aggression, with Satan wanting to disperse the little company of Jesus' followers. But instead of saying, "I pray for you all" as might have been expected, Jesus speaks only of His prayer for Peter, the *one,* that his faith might not fail. For if this faith remains firm because of Jesus' prayer, then the attack directed against all of them is repelled. They will all be steadfast in the faith, strengthened by the *one.* In Matthew 16:22-23, we see how very powerfully Satan tempts only this *one* apostle. Right after Simon had been chosen as "the rock" he aspired to surpass even Jesus, suggesting that his own will prevail, but Jesus commanded the tempter to leave, and ordered His disciple to take his place behind Him and to follow Him until death. According to Jesus, both Peter and all the others should be mindful only of the things that are of God, and not the things that are of men.

After Christ had instituted powers of authority for the people of the New Covenant, He pronounced the words, *"It is finished"* upon the cross. This authority was confirmed by the Father in the resurrection of His Son, and during the Forty Days the Risen One sealed this institution of authority in His Kingdom, an authority that no slander, flight, sin or death could ever destroy. The first of all the disciples to whom Christ appeared was Peter, *the Rock.* It was the Apostle Paul who informed the Corinthians (I Cor. 15:5) regarding the order observed in the Lord's appearances. Exalted by the grace of God, the Lord brought His Church into existence not only by virtue of His authority as the incarnate and crucified Shepherd, but with an authority that was eternal and included the authority of all the redeemed, and of all who exercised leadership, and the authority of the *one.* In the Gospel of

John, 21:2, the disciples are mentioned in a group of seven as a figure of oneness for the Church, as also for the members of the New Covenant *ecclesia* of Israel and the nations, even as "the Twelve" had primarily referred to the twelve tribes of Israel.

In John 21 the form of the order of authority, with the *one* at the helm, is clearly discernible as a revelation of enduring significance. Even as the Forty Days pointed toward the entire Christian era of our salvation, the Fourth Gospel in its final, supplemental chapter likewise refers entirely to the development of the Church's history "until His coming again." Again and again the verbs change from the past to the present tense and the span of the arc extends from the beginning to the end of the Gospel, for as *rock* had previously indicated royal status in the Old Covenant and among the nations, and as the "keeper of the keys" was the successor of King David and the custodian of his everlasting throne, so too the *Shepherd* is the ruler of the nation forever. The promised Messias was also described as the one who would feed the people of God (Mt. 2:6; Jn. 21:15). Jesus therefore handed His pastoral staff to one of the disciples in order that all the redeemed might be one flock under one shepherd. There must be *one* who guards and protects us all from the devil who is our persecutor. The *one* must watch over the weak and the small, and direct those who are strong, serving all men so that they may have life and full happiness in the Lord. The shepherd's service is consequently an act of love, a return of love to Him who first loved Christ and all mankind. It is the bond of Jesus' love, and of the love of God and the brethren, which holds the entire Church together indissolubly. This all-embracing service of the Shepherd is also extended to his fellow pastors, the priests and bishops of the Church. Elsewhere in John 21 we see that this Church celebrates the one Lord's Supper. She undertakes a universal missionary work which owes all of its progress and blessing to the presence of the Lord. There is *one* who brings about the great ingathering of fish in the last days. There is *one* who pulls the net onto the land. The devil cannot destroy the walled pen of the flock and the fishnet does not break. Neither will the building which God has built ever fall apart. In John 1:41-42, regarding the *WORD,* we learn that it is the *WORD* who is the bearer of the *rock* and of all those who believe that Jesus is the Christ, the Son of God, possessing life in His name through this faith.

Faith! Life! But can we also claim that the bearers of Jesus' authority possess some kind of legal right, or even a divine right, *jus divinum?* Does this institution of authority, as applied to the Church of the New Testament, have to be made into an everlasting Law? Someone will object, "A return to the Law! A legal interpretation of the Gospel!" It is however the teaching of the Gospel that the Church of the New Covenant came forth from the creative act of the *WORD* and continues to exist through that same *WORD.* When this truth is proclaimed, we are also proclaiming the form of the Church and the institution of her authority. God protects what He has created and He makes His action known to us all in order that we may believe and have life. It is by God's decree that the Church endures, but God's decree is the law of God (the Latin "fas"). Even the rulers of this world base their authority upon the law of God. The Old Covenant was one of law. The New Covenant, however, is superior to the Old in regard to both divine decree and divine law, for the law of Christ and of His Kingdom is for all time and for eternity. If this were not so, the Church could not claim the right to existence and would be suppressed by the claims of other legal powers. But the Church is within the compass of His Law, for the Lord calls her "My Church." He possesses her by right of ownership.

"Feed *my* lambs . . . feed *my* sheep!" says the great Shepherd of the flock. We see, therefore, that the Lord *possesses property*. He came unto His own, with authority from His Father, and through His sacrificial death He has legitimately acquired us all. In the Son of God and Son of Man there is every divine and human law in full measure. If He authorizes someone to be the guardian of His property, both divine and human law become effective in the exercise of that person's vocation. If we made no reference to the New Testament at all, it could be said that the Law of the Shepherd and of the entire Church was without validity, and then Christians, young and old, could no longer claim the loving care of Christ who gives them corporate unity through the chief pastor (and his fellow pastors). The law of God serves life, and is the internal and external Law of Life for the Church which was called into existence by God. The law and authority of the chief pastor and his fellow pastors will endure as long as there are people who believe in Jesus and wish to belong to Him as "God's chosen people." The word *testament* also expresses the continuing existence of the Church's order as shown in the New Testament. The decree of God and the Law is set forth in Jesus' last will. Who can contest or annul it? Our temporal and eternal life rests upon the Law of His Person and His office. Within the order of His kingdom all the members of the kingdom possess their right to life. Outside of the fold, the fishnet, the building, the temple, the king's palace, the people and the body of

Jesus Christ, and apart from the work and word of the One who has acquired us as His own through death and resurrection, we would all remain in death. But since we are baptized into His death, His life has become our own.

We must not lose sight of this truth, especially now that the revelation concerning the shepherd is becoming clearer to us again. Through holy baptism all Christians are embodied into Christ as the Second Adam and consequently they are delivered from the first Adam's domain of death. They are brought into the kingdom of Jesus' order and power, and into a filial relationship with God the Father, with all of its rights and responsibilities. We are transplanted into the very life of Jesus and consequently we are His own by virtue of our nature, as lambs and sheep of His pasture, entrusted to the shepherd He has chosen. It is according to God's order that we are led and fed by Jesus, and it is God's will that we have a legal right to this care, precisely in keeping with the pastoral authority which was established by the Son of God, and this right cannot be lost. We should study the entire New Testament to determine the kind of law and authority denounced and rejected by the Lord as being a law of coercion in accord with royal majesty and the tyrants of this world. The Law of the New Covenant was no longer to be that of the "servants" of the Old Covenant. It is instead the law of the Father-and-son relationship, and therefore a law of love, with the status of brotherhood. This Law is the very strongest, immeasurably stronger than anything else in the domain of law, for the first-born of all the brethren has accepted us as brothers, and the children of God remain eternally in the Father's House. Our status as children of the Father, obtained for us through the Son of God, is everlasting. For it is love which makes us participants in the life of God.

It is through superabundant grace that we are already participating by faith in the life of God the Father, Son and Holy Spirit, and therefore everything which confronts the Church militant here on earth in her journey and struggle is illumined by the Church triumphant in heaven, where those who have won the victory are reigning in the holy ranks of the heavenly hierarchy and are a kingdom. They lay down their crowns before the Lamb and worship with Him, their High Priest for all eternity, in the adoration of the Father. As those who have persevered in the faith they are witnesses of the victory of the eternal Gospel. It is by this heavenly worship that the eternal order of supreme power influences the world below, intervening in the struggles of the Church and the course of history. To those who are victorious in the struggle there will be the same fellowship with the triumphant Lord in the glory of God (Apocalypse of John and the Epistle to the Hebrews).

The Law of God is apparent in creation and in the Church. We are encompassed by it even if we never acknowledge it, or do so in a merely partial way. However, if we are willing, hereafter, to acknowledge the order and authority of the Church in accordance with the Gospel, and without reservation, our divisions will diminish. It is through God's living Word that everything which is divisive can be overcome.

We should consider Melanchthon's testimony concerning the primacy of the pope, by human right, "for the sake of peace and general unity" which is not without importance in these times when the last pillars of established order in our compressed world, and the very existence of man are concerned. However, only the man who recognizes God as God, through whose grace the priestly king Jesus Christ established the divine order here on earth, can be saved because he has been "pardoned." This man alone has been saved and becomes the savior of his fellow-men. It is divine law alone which makes the Church of all believers a unity, in order that the Church, through her oneness, may become a new witness of the living Savior in the world of men.

There is an important significance for us sons of the Reformation in Martin Luther's call to prayer and prophecy in matters pertaining to the pope as Peter's successor, when he declared in the year 1519 at the debate in Leipzig, "I ask Doctor Eck, therefore, that he call on the name of the Lord Jesus Christ with me, to impart not only to the chief bishop, but to all bishops, a willingness to apply to themselves the words of 'the Gospel of the shepherd in Jesus' place, John 21' for there is no doubt that the whole world would receive such a man, conducting himself according to these teachings, with open arms and warm tears of joy."

This also was a Reformation point of view. It could now at last prevail among us. However, the decisive factor is whether God Himself has opened the Scriptures to us in regard to the order and authority of His Church. And He definitely *has* opened them to us now. What are the consequences to be? What does God command? "Ye men and beloved brethren, what are we to do?"

HANS ASMUSSEN

CATHOLIC TRUTH, TRADITION
AND MINISTRY

"The Christian life is almost inconceivably simple. We give ourselves into the keeping of God and of Christ, and everything else will be added to us in due time." This is a true statement, but it leaves a good deal unsaid. Anyone whose knowledge of Christianity is limited to such a statement, and who teaches others no more than this, is not telling the whole truth and is tempting himself as well as others. "For the Christian life is also very complex. It is a complexity of relationships which appears to an outsider as utterly confusing." This kind of statement is likewise true, and yet each of these statements is false if our knowledge and teaching are limited to only one of them. The wisdom of Christianity is found in affirming both truths at appropriate times and with the proper emphasis.

Perhaps this can be clarified by way of example. Anyone going from Kiel to Moscow must travel eastward. If we give this kind of information to the traveler, we are advising and directing him correctly. But if we say no more than that, we have informed him poorly, for in reality a trip to Moscow is a very complicated matter that can be completed only in successive stages. This simple illustration, however inadequate, does nevertheless clearly emphasize the importance of realizing that man, in his life, cannot forego basic directions, which contain the whole of Christian life. If, however, man assumes that any of these constitute the whole, he is quite mistaken. The particular directions are necessary, and in combination they result in the one whole. This is applicable to the Church and the Scriptures, the ministry and ecclesiastical leadership. The whole must not be left out of sight any more than the particular part together with the relationships between the individual components.

1. We can regard the Christian life as the way of salvation, leading the individual to eternal life. There are sayings of our Lord which teach us to ignore everything around us if only we can save our souls. Since the salvation of the individual is a legitimate Christian concern and also a legitimate life-purpose for a Christian, the Church of Christ can claim that it points out the way, and is itself the way, wherein the individual finds his true self. It would be inadmissible if the Church were ever to forget this. But if we now pursue the question further and ask how the individual can attain to his salvation, we will find that with every step he takes he will encounter other people who are also walking in this same way of salvation, and he cannot pass them without also seeing or meeting them. In order to find his true self, he must sooner or later find the others. And these others, who are also seeking salvation, have likewise come to believe in Jesus Christ. We will not now refer to those who are unbelieving, who may even be closely related to us, but we shall have to consider them later. For the present we are concerned only about these other Christians. It is in clarifying our relationship with them that our relationship to ourselves is properly founded. These other Christians include both the living who are among us today, and also those who, from the beginning of the Christian Church, have departed this present life before us. Of this vast number

of living and departed Christians there are some who are
of special importance and are of particular concern to ourselves. We must determine who they are. As a result, for
the Christian, neither the present or past is a confused
mass of people. For it happens that in distinguishing one-
self from others one discovers himself.

All of this pertains to the Church as well. Her self-seek-
ing is an essential aspect of her ecclesiastical life. In Wür-
temberg I was commenting upon certain ecclesiastical
matters relating to Bremen, and suddenly one of the pastors interrupted me, asking, "What does Bremen matter
to us?" An attitude of this kind is forbidden to the Church.
We cannot overlook any fellowship of believers anywhere
in this world who call themselves a "church." Nor can we
exclude any of the centuries of the past, for the Church
must seek her very self in all of them. The platonic explanation that there must always have been a true church
somewhere, is not satisfactory. We must ask specifically:
What was the Church like in the past? Who stood in
Christ's place in the Church of those days? We need to
remember that the Church has always been ecumenical
both in her depth and her extent. It is this ecumenical aspect which is closely related to the incarnation of Christ.
The Son of God truly appeared in the form of man. One
could always point back toward a certain person in history
and say, "He is the Son of God." However, this could not
be done without faith, but if one were believing, this
statement could be made, and it would then be possible
to behold His glory. Those who were without faith also
beheld the Son of God in the son of Man, but for them it
was as though seeing, they saw not. However, since the
ascension of Jesus Christ into heaven, leaving His Church

in the world to represent Him, the marvellous extension
of the incarnation has been apparent at all times.

We can point to the Church, as to the Son of God, and
say, "There is the true Church." But this, also, requires
faith. Nevertheless, it is something we ought to do. Those
who are without faith will also behold the Body of Christ,
and yet they will see it not, for the eyes of the unbelieving
are deceived.

Obviously there are two extremes to be avoided. We
should not speak of the visibleness of the Church as though
faith were not needed to perceive her as the Body of
Christ. The Roman Catholic Church has at times been in
danger of this erroneous extreme. Nor should we say that
it can simply be assumed that the true Church is now to
be found in this place or that, since we must believe that
the Church does exist and must therefore exist somewhere.
The Lutheran Church is especially prone to this kind of
error, and has often taken this position leading to the
false doctrine of an invisible church, which has been very
detrimental.

The existence of Christ's Church cannot be demonstrated as self-evident. However, the Church's presence
among us can and should be affirmed through the testimony of witnesses. People should be told specifically to
go here or go there to find the Body of our Lord Jesus
Christ. The warning of our Lord against listening to those
who say, "Behold, Christ is here or He is there!" is not
applicable in regard to the Church, for this warning will
not hinder the quest for the true Church but will instead
clearly emphasize that error and temptation are always
possible in the quest.

2. In our search for the Church, however, we must especially seek for the authentic signs of Christian life, includ-

ing the Church's achievements and her sufferings. This will bring us into contact with those whom Catholic piety calls the *saints*. For it is they who have formed the very face of the Church through their good deeds and their afflictions. It is therefore of great importance that we never lose our relationship to the martyrs of our own time but rather seek to establish it. This has been sadly neglected since 1945 in regard to Eastern countries. Leading ecclesiastical groups in the West did not want to offend the statesmen of the East, and consequently there was a conspiracy of silence concerning the martyrs. A notable and praiseworthy exception was the attitude of the Lutheran Church concerning Bishop Ordass, and likewise the testimony of the Church in other countries and other eras. We want to know how Christian truth was understood in past centuries and in different lands. The present interest in church history and dogma and ecclesiology are not mere hobbies of certain scholars, but are the necessary outpouring of the Christian spirit. In the testimony of others we are really seeking the Lord of the Church Himself, just as we search for Him in the sufferings and the activities of the Church. We have therefore no choice as to where we will do our seeking. All the centuries and all countries will be of interest to us.

The accomplishments of the ecumenical movement since the days of Nathan Söderblom must be mentioned in this connection. While the movement pertains to the Church of the present time, it is nevertheless astounding to consider what has been happening in the Evangelical world during the past thirty years. It must be admitted, however, that the search for the Church in its Catholic form has been neglected by Lutherans both with regard to the present and the past. The anti-Catholic complex is certainly not yet overcome. Among Catholics there has been opposition to the movement, as is commonly known. But things have really started to move. The institute for the study of denominational doctrines which the Catholics established in Paderborn, and a similar institute which the Lutheran Churches are planning to open, are indications of this change. There are many other evidences of favorable attitude toward the movement, and some are highly important. We are beginning to acquire the courage to learn about one another through personal witness and not merely through our own polemical literature. For ourselves, this means a full realization that the history of the Church did not have its beginning in 1517. In seeking our Lord Jesus Christ, we must listen for His voice in those departed Christians who lived before 1517. It is not our vocation to be merely the representatives of a "reformed theology." Our Lord is calling us to an understanding of the theology of all the preceding centuries. Everything that has occurred in the Christian Church since the death of Christ in regard to doctrine and teaching is binding upon us. A life-giving stream has come down to us as "tradition" and during the 1900 years that have passed since the first council of the apostles there has been a living stream of living testimony concerning the gospel, to which all of us are indebted. In bringing this stream of tradition into prominence we must warn against the spirit of absolutism which was characteristic of the sixteenth century. However, the voices of that century must not be omitted either.

The question also arises regarding the attitude to be taken when we realize that in the long history of the Church the waters of this stream have often seemed to be flowing uphill, or were actually doing so. It can now be affirmed that some of the controversies of the past were based upon misunderstandings, but certainly not all of them. Each generation must determine for itself how far it can confirm the decisions made in preceding centuries. But such an inquiry always results in new divisions within the Church and Christendom. The Lutheran criticism of the Catholic Church of the sixteenth century, for instance, is not in any way applicable to the Catholic Church of our day. This is just as obvious as the fact that the critical position of contemporary Catholic theologians simply does not apply to Martin Luther nor to the Lutheran theology or Lutheran Church of the present time. The current task is therefore to make a careful analysis of our position, and determine what must be retained and what should be given up for the sake of truth.

3. This fundamental stand must be attained primarily because the New Testament in no way presents an obvious unanimity concerning details, and the Catholic declaration which we often hear, assuring us that there can be only one truth, is quite as definitely an over-simplification as the Lutheran statement that the unity of the Church is to be found in unity of doctrine. There is something true in both statements, of course, but each becomes a heresy when presented as an absolute. Is there, for instance, a *consensus de doctrina evangelii* in the Lutheran Church of the Missouri Synod between professors Künneth, Schlink, Peter Brunner, Nygren and Skydsgaard? There is such a consensus and yet there is not. The formula is therefore only partially correct. Who would deny that Rome possesses remarkable skill in "interpreting" the dogmatic formulas of the past? And who would be so unrealistic as to make accusations against Rome because of it? The declaration that the unity of the Church is based

upon unity of doctrine is quite as divisive as the statement assuring us that there is only one truth. When we realize that these divisive formulas are matters of controversy we are simply experiencing bewilderment and seeing through a glass darkly (I Cor. 13). The real harm lies in the fact that the impression is created that a dogma of the Church, officially promulgated is not subject to further development since it is a premature declaration of what will only be truly revealed in the world to come. Is this an expression of relativism? Only a lack of understanding would prompt us to say *yes* with insistence. The fear of relativism is justified both among Catholics and among Lutherans. But this fear, and relativism itself, cannot be overcome by trying to create the impression that there exists a degree of doctrinal unity or explicit truth which can never be surpassed in this world. St. John of the Cross and the great St. Teresa barely avoided being condemned for their teachings. In this present world the utterance of great truths will always exceed the defined limits of doctrine. By way of contrast we could mention the Lutheran theology of the seventeenth century. It was engaged in controversy concerning the propriety of attributing absolute omnipresence to the risen Christ or merely an omnipresence according to His will. In that day there were theologians who believed in the validity of the principle of church unity through the *consensus de doctrina evangelii* in spite of this difference in theological teaching. This was manifestly erroneous, but can any remedy be suggested for this condition?

4. Fortunately there is indeed a remedy! First of all, there is prayer for wisdom, for which we are to ask (James 1). But that is not all. Christian truth must be presented as something based upon impersonal and idealistic au-

thority. In this sense Christian truth exists even apart from those who are its bearers and teachers, but this question has never yet been fully clarified for Christians. There is, of course, something undoubtedly akin to that "form of doctrine" (Rom. 6:17) to which all Christians must be obedient. On the other hand, this form of doctrine must be clearly distinguished from philosophical ideas, chiefly because the doctrine comes from God and it pleased Him to conjoin it everlastingly with a certain people and their destiny. Christ said, "He who hears you, hears me" (Lk. 10:16). In this way He committed the teaching of Christian truth to persons holding a particular office, and while Christian truth is never found apart from the office, we must remember that the office itself is inseparable from the mission of Christ, and consequently Christian truth does exist eternally apart from the persons appointed to teach it. That is why the history of Christian truth is much more than a history of ideas. In this respect the position of the Lutheran Reformers was reactionary when they separated the doctrine from the teaching ministry, for the "form of doctrine" that exists independently of persons is nevertheless conjoined with the ministry and comes forth through them as the history of Christian truth. This point of view protects us from the absolutism of the doctrine.

In regard to this question evangelical theology has unintentionally contributed a great deal. The Reformers and their opponents both understood the Scriptures in a rather superficial manner. I myself was brought up on the theology of the Concordance which taught us to pursue one concept throughout the entire Bible on the assumption that each text would prove that the meaning was always the same. Evangelical theology however also laid stress on identifying each concept with the person who referred to it. For example, if it was the concept of "righteousness," we would have to determine what meaning Paul gave to this term, or John, etc. The New Testament is consequently in itself the testimony of a history, but this knowledge is confusing. It appears once again to lead toward relativism. Which one of the many Apostles shall we take for our guide? Should we not be thankful to God if there be a Pope—or an Evangelical Faculty—to relieve us of this decision? But it does not really happen this way, for we all make our decisions according to the office or talent which we have received, and yet the Church asks us if we are willing to accept *her* decision.

5. We cannot therefore take our stand upon any particular interpretation of the Bible. The hiatus between exegesis and dogma, so prevalent in our time, is not a healthy condition. Who would deny that in both the Catholic and Protestant Churches exegesis and dogma now exist like a married couple who have agreed upon separation from bed and board. If the Lutheran Church accepted the conclusions offered to her by the exegesis of Schlatter and by modern commentators, there would be a sudden change in Lutheran dogma. It may also be affirmed that revisions could be made in Catholic dogma if the Catholic Church were to draw conclusions from what Catholic commentators have learned in their study of Evangelical exegesis.

How does the Bible appear to us today? Exegesis has disintegrated into a confusing welter of particular convictions. The commentator refers to "righteousness according to Paul" without giving us a simultaneous and binding concept of righteousness. The dogmatist meanwhile tells us what Luther and the Lutheran creeds meant by "justification" and makes this interpretation obligatory.

It is my impression that matters are not very different in
the Catholic Church, even though the new Catholic cat-
echism has clarified and harmonized much of this. However, we cannot do justice either to Christian truth or to
the heritage of Christian history until we bring exegesis
and dogma together again. The future relationship between our own churches, and between the Catholic and
Evangelical Church, depends upon the solution of this
problem. The difficulty lies in the fact that modern exegesis is being pursued upon a scientific basis while our
dogmatics have developed upon a foundation which cannot be described as scientific. Neither the Lutheran creeds
nor the canons of Trent questioned the expression of
Biblical truth in Paul, Matthew or John. In the fullest
sense the religious world of the different books of the
Bible was unknown when those creeds and canons were
formed, and consequently exegesis was undertaken without a scientific foundation. Can we now return to the
exegesis of our forefathers in any way whatever? If this
were possible, should we forego the scientific basis of our
own exegesis? In my opinion, we ought to combine our
inherited ecclesiastical method with the scientific method.
It is not, however, only a question of method, for the special quality of Christian existence manifests itself.

In *one* point both the Augsburg Confession and the
canons of the Council of Trent are in agreement against
the attitude of our time. Both regard the Scriptures as
"inspired" documents. By this term they mean that God
Himself, through the Holy Spirit, speaks to us directly in
Holy Scripture. According to both interpretations, it is
best to read each biblical author in such a way that the
historical aspect should never be of essential importance
to us since God is expressing Himself through these testi-

monies in an unmediated manner. As a matter of fundamental principle all biblical scholars applied the allegorical method of interpretation, for instance, and until the newer exegesis came into existence both Catholics and Protestants used this method without hesitation. Nevertheless, it was simply an historical phenomenon. In this kind of exegesis the conviction is expressed that we are not merely dealing with historical, literary testimony in these biblical records but with divine Scripture. We are not mistaken in assuming that this point of view has a very minor role, or perhaps no role whatever, in modern exegesis. This clearly indicates that both Catholics and Protestants of our day consider the scientific method as irreconcilable with, for instance, Paul's way of regarding Holy Scripture. This constitutes a vital theological problem and influences the attitudes and relations between the Churches to some extent.

The dilemma certainly is profound. We must determine whether the old method of interpretation of Scripture was fully cognizant of the human character of the Scriptures. It must be conceded that the human aspect has been studied in an unprecedented manner by the modern exegetical method. Luther's attempt, on the other hand, to erect biblical time-posts, which required an endless amount of effort, was based upon the belief that the Scriptures impart absolutely reliable historical information because of their divine character. Modern exegetical methods, however, in no way suggest that the exegete is aware of anything divine in the character of the Bible, a character that would even pertain to the very letter of Scripture (Gal. 3:16). However, the dogma accepted in both the Catholic and Protestant Churches exists wholly in the world of the old exegesis.

6. Agreement can only be reached when the Christian teaching office is accorded its full prerogatives in a practical way. Evangelical weakness lies in the depersonification of the doctrine, but it must be said that centralization within the Roman Catholic Church no longer provides an effective remedy against this kind of weakness. How did our Protestant depersonification of doctrine originate? It was precisely because early medieval bishops ceased to be teachers and left the teaching office to professors. The Reformation did not occur during an era when bishops were teaching the faith. This development, however, was only possible because the bishops had deprived themselves of much authority in favor of the papacy, and the papacy was itself depriving the bishops of episcopal power. Tasks were left to the professors which they were unable to accomplish. It is not a question of learned research with regard to the ability to combine the dual aspect of biblical testimony into a single unity, but concerns the teaching office itself. The bishop is the teacher of his diocese while also governing it and representing it as a successor of Christ in the office of high priest. The professor's function is auxiliary. Everything is bound to go badly if the bishop refuses to exercise any part of his episcopal authority. He cannot delegate to others the representation of Christ in his diocese in regard to the teaching office, or administration, or the priestly office, except in auxiliary capacities, because the representation of Christ is a totality and a unity. The error of the Reformation concerning Holy Scripture did not consist so much in particular dogmas, as in making Christian truth independent of the teaching office. It claimed that a *successio* of the *doctrina* existed in and by itself, and that this *successio* was self-sufficient. However, the apostolicity of the Church is not so much

an historical question in the sense that it need only be shown that the Church is derived from the twelve apostles. Apostolicity consists primarily in the preservation of the apostolic office as a succession of Christ in the exercise of the high priesthood, the teaching office and leadership. It then possesses decisive consequences in regard to the Scriptures, for we cannot regard them as merely a collection of truths. The New Testament is primarily and always a triad of doctrine and testimony, congregational leadership and priestly service. (We need only remember Paul's detailed comments on prayer!) In view of all this, we cannot simply designate the theological content of the New Testament as traditional. If modern exegesis rightly points out that each New Testament writing had a particular message (consider, for example, the Gnostics to whom the Epistle of the Colossians refers), we cannot therefore conclude that an abstraction of the special motive of the Epistle will reveal the abstract and everlasting scriptural content. It would be preferable to conclude that Scripture in the New Testament presents a process by which the form of the Christian Church was being fashioned. When post-apostolic generations considered the Scriptures in the light of faith, they did not regard them as a collection of abstract truths but rather as a record of the doctrinal process which was begun by the apostles.

7. In this light we can understand how and why the ancient Councils required a particular bishop to declare his personal credo which was then judged by the collective episcopate in regard to the orthodoxy of the bishop. For the new situation (new in relation to the New Testament) demanded not only the decision of a particular bishop concerning the matter in question, but also the judgment of the corporate body as to whether the doctrinal history

begun in the first generation could be continued through this individual bishop. In this respect the credo of the particular bishop, and the subsequent credo of the collective episcopate, were also a summary of lasting truths. It is necessary to realize this clearly because it constitutes a condensation of ecclesiastical history, making it a history of doctrine.

The Reformers diminished the historical process in regard to doctrine even further by their involuntary abolition of the episcopal office. Thereafter it was only the professor and the abstract, isolated doctrine that remained. It is only in this sense that we can understand how, after four hundred years, the professor of our day has become a pure scientist (like Harnack, for instance) who, having neither the obligation nor the desire to make doctrinal decisions for the Church, now initiates inquiries into matters of church history and controversial theological opinions, even though he may be unquestionably motivated by a lofty ethos. We must wait to see what has been developing since 1945. It often seems apparent that a healthy counter-movement is under way, but there are times when the observer finds it painful to note that many professors are again returning to the position prevalent in 1925 and consequently produce a "theology" which even fails to reach the viewpoint of professors of the seventeenth century.

What is the situation in the Roman Catholic Church? The dogma that the office of a teacher belongs to the bishop is apparently undisputed. Nevertheless, this dogma is often weakened not merely because of human imperfections, but also because of a dominant centralism. If we Lutherans find that comments by theologians and laymen in any country are being contested in Roman Catholic statements without prior discussion with the bishop or even in direct contrast to his decision, we inevitably get the impression that an important principle of Catholicism has been over-ridden or perhaps abandoned entirely. It was gratifying that the Pope at one time reprimanded Bismarck for his accusation that Catholic bishops, after the Vatican Council, had become mere functionaries of the Holy See. However, we can only regret everything which Bismarck could later justify in his accusations. We Lutherans may certainly envy the Catholic Church's advantage in her emphatic rejection of false doctrine, but Roman centralism has made this advantage questionable. What is our real objection in this matter? We will not make our answer in the spirit of relativistic Protestantism, for there is no reason for us to do so. But it is necessary that we stress the importance of completing the reformation of the Christian Church without interference, and this depends upon a universal respect for opposite opinions wherever the Christian Church exists. If a controversial question has not been decided upon within the area of a bishopric, it should not be suppressed by the Church anywhere in the world. This is not a matter of established prerogatives—although it is that also—but a pastoral question. Truth cannot be controlled; it can only be affirmed in the priestly office. If truth is isolated from priesthood, there is a destruction of both the priesthood as well as the office of the teacher. Among Lutherans there has certainly been a realization of what occurs when the teaching office becomes absolute. That is our reason for mentioning it here.

8. It may be protested from the Catholic side, and quite rightly, that the world-wide Catholic Church cannot possibly be concerned about the witness of particular dioceses

because of the special demands of universality, although this might be possible within a union of Churches that are exclusively German (the German Evangelical Church, for example.) We can only agree with this objection to a certain extent. It is certainly true that in our German Evangelical Church we still lack experience in coping with the contrasting patterns of a South American bishopric and a German diocese. But something significant can nevertheless be said against this objection. Evangelical Churches, and especially the Lutheran Church, have proved that it is possible to establish direct connections beyond national boundaries without jeopardizing the the central authority. The weaknesses of a system like that of the Evangelical Church in Germany are obvious, but it should be kept always in mind that this system, compared with the Catholic dioceses in Germany, provides certain advantages also. Primarily there is a real independence in freedom, happily conjoined with cooperation, which is not similarly found in the Catholic dioceses. This can be achieved, however, only when the centralization is circumscribed in principle, and this is an unescapable note or trait of Catholicity. Roman Catholics, including their leaders in high places, are far ahead of us Lutherans in willing and praying for the unity of Christendom. But if we ask them what kind of unity they have in mind, we are generally told rather timidly that they are thinking in terms of our conversion. Now, we certainly do not intend to burden anyone's conscience, for when a person has decided to become a convert, nothing further can properly be said. However, conversion is not the solution of the problem of the Churches. Nor does it point the way toward attainment of Christian unity. It cannot be otherwise, for the obvious reason that the gifts of the Spirit, which Evangelical Christians do not deny to the Catholic Church, and which Catholics admittedly recognize in the Evangelical Churches, must not be permitted to be lost.

If we had all advanced to the point that both sides would consider it a legitimate question to consider what things in our own traditions should not be abandoned, we would have progressed much farther than is the case today. And this is precisely a matter of Catholicity, combining the will to unity with the will to live in our own way. The primitive church in Jerusalem, according to Acts 15, followed this very course, acknowledging the unity of all Christians in accordance with the declarations of the apostles, and yet making a decision in regard to the requirements that should be made of those whose Christian life had not been formed by the traditions of the church in Jerusalem.

9. We must strive for an episcopal office that will see in a particular diocese an ecclesiastical body in which the living Christian development is taking place, and is especially being fulfilled because the individual diocese with its bishop is content to be only a part of the whole. This also implies recognition of the layman and of his voice in the whole life and growth of the Church. This certainly does not mean that the spiritual office of the clergy, or even of the bishop, should be reduced to a mere function of the lay society, but it is extremely important that there be no sharp contrast between the clergy and laity. Calvinistic churches are suspected of a democratic misunderstanding of the function of the ministry and especially the episcopate. However, no one will seriously claim that the Lutheran and Catholic Churches allow the voice of the laity to be really heard, or that we have nothing further to learn in this respect. Our synods, although originally

formed according to the Calvinist pattern, certainly cannot pretend to permit the expression of lay opinion, but rather tend to minimize any opposition between clergy and laity.

Whatever may be said concerning lay persons will involve us in questions pertaining to the selection and appointment of ministers. This was given mention in the earliest Lutheran theological writings. Nor should the lay point of view be dismissed from consideration. But we must not overlook other elements pertaining to the real origins of the ministry simply because of the participation of the laity. No special proof need be cited to show that it was not in accordance with the gospel when, in former days, the Roman nobility selected the pope. It is even more intolerable that the court chamberlain of the Byzantine Emperor or the Czar of Russia (or even the chairman of the Communist Party in Moscow) could appoint the Eastern Patriarchs. This allowed the Church of God no participation whatever in the selection of her spiritual shepherds. The determination of the papacy in extricating itself from political powers is deserving of our appreciation. For it cannot be said that our own system of appointing bishops is particularly desirable. It has been found that it definitely results in the production of "Grey Eminences." But the fundamental principle itself must not be set aside, for a part of our spiritual life is dependent upon it.

In this chapter some lost Catholic truths have been pointed out. They have been presented primarily and properly for the attention of Evangelical Christians. Perhaps, however, Roman Catholics will consider them also. I have no "Catholicizing" inclinations but rather a passion for Catholicity. That is why I seek the fellowship of all believers in Christ, whether of our own time or those of the past. Consequently it is my hope that I will hear the teaching voice of the Church of the present day, counselling and judging through God's own Word. I also realize that I am subject to the authority of the Church when her decisions are made in these times, and for that same reason, also, I want to submit to all the decisions which the Church has made in the past, and I must therefore know which of these past decisions are binding upon me. Whatever is binding is my strength and support.

WOLFGANG LEHMANN

THE SIGNIFICANCE OF LOST CATHOLIC TRUTHS FOR THE LIFE OF THE CHURCH

The Confessional Synod in Barmen (1934) was the decisive turning-point for a renewal of the German Evangelical Church. It would be well to recall the "Exposition of the *practical* work of the Confessional Synod of the German Evangelical Church," which was determined on that occasion and was set forth in the sixth thesis of the "Theological Manifesto."

"The task of the Church, in which her freedom is founded, consists in bringing the message of the free grace of God to the whole human race, in Christ's stead and likewise in the service of His own Word and Work through sermon and sacrament." Before the Synod accepted the thesis introduced and presented in these terms, the following statement was being presented in the form of a motion:

". . . . . the Lutheran scholar, Vilmar, was able to foresee the characteristic trends of the present hour. In the year 1851, he had already expressed the fear that in the following decades, and in a progressive manner (i.e., in an accelerated tempo) the substance from which the Churches, and more especially the pastoral ministry were being sustained, would be wholly exhausted. He saw this substance in the vanishing stages both in the natural temperament of the German people as their history had formed them, and secondly, in the Christianization of this natural temperament, and he could foresee the approaching time when the process of Christianization would weaken and eventually collapse. He predicted that the Christianized element itself would falter and perish. In this natural element Vilmar perceived certain vital forces of natural origin: the desire for family, the desire for domestic stability, the desire for community status and recognition, and the desires for naturalness and for honor and other qualities. . . ." I believe that Cyprian once said, "Only he who has the Church for his mother can have God for his Father." This is a good Catholic statement and also a good Evangelical statement. It was one of the delegates to the Synod in Barmen who made these remarks.

We can deduce two significant inferences: 1) the Church has begun to balance the books and to face the fact that the majority of her members have been swept along into apostasy in an ever-increasing manner from generation to generation. 2) The Church is once more beginning to reveal herself as a mother, and conduct herself as a sheltering haven and liberating force even in these times of widespread apostasy.

I

The problem of man's spiritual condition in our time requires that we see man and society in a period of apostasy, with all the symptoms of a sick and divided soul, and among all these apostates only a small minority of believers. Analyses of the sick condition of the individual as well as of society may be found in many books and other publications, but Vilmar's prophesy might be sufficient in regard to this. The conference in Barmen performed a much more profound operation upon the sick body of Protestantism than a mere deliverance of the Church from the attitudes and influences of National Socialism (although many Lutherans were of the opinion, and still believe, that nothing more was at stake than this question of defense). The courage for a realistic understanding of the situation, together with the stand taken by the multitude of baptized people in their religious faith, can be attributed to the renewal of the Evangelical Churches.

Vilmar's prophetic view concerning the "crumbling and breakdown of the Christianizing process, and the perishing of the Christianized elements" is considerably more realistic today than it was in the year 1934. For the generation who belonged to *Bekennenden Kirche* * in that period continued, although in a diminished manner, to adhere to the "Christianized natural instincts" (family, honesty, authority, etc.). The present generation, however, which is the bearer of our public life, has entirely forgotten and forsaken the virtues mentioned by Vilmar, not to speak of the appreciation and realization of those virtues. We must also remember that this shrinking process is occurring at a time when a "world-wide historical caesura of the first magnitude has taken place, its vast effect probably comparable only to man's change to stationary ways of life in the beginning of the Neolithic Era. The construction of machines, and making them work at his command, while becoming profoundly dependent upon their pace and performance, has been a revolution that changed the whole life of man as thoroughly as the earlier decision to live within four walls and identify his destiny with that

* That part of the German Evangelical Church which refused to give in to Nationalistic pressures.

of a piece of ground to be cultivated like a garden." [1] The diminution of all Christian virtues in an environment that has become a completely altered milieu, and in a new world of transformed concepts and images, is an observation which makes us ask whether the means by which the Church tries to reach such enslaved and blinded people and to lead them to salvation through Jesus Christ, are really in keeping with the task and in any way effective. But they will only be so (and most thoroughly!) when they are fully in compliance with the order and will of the Lord and are thus pleasing to God. It is not their "success" or "failure" which will then be the criterion of their appropriateness and power, but rather their quality as the means of grace actually bearing and offering Christ and His salvation. The continuously increasing failure of the Church among people of whom ninety per cent are apostates, could perhaps be connected with the *Cross of Christ*. However, we cannot make such a reference to Christ's Cross when the Church's failure is due to the fact that man has changed and has diminished God's means of salvation. When our best and most faithful Church members become fully resigned to this situation, it is an alarming sign which should be seriously recognized by the Church. A sincere, general examination to determine whether the "means of grace" are also being offered and administered in accordance with the intention of the Lord is at the same time one of the most important considerations in the Church's endeavor to reach outsiders, if there is to be any assurance of success. Better than any analysis deduced from experience, we find in Luke 11:24-26 the kind of subjection in which both individual men and society find themselves

[1] Hans Freyer: *Theorie des gegenwärtigen Zeitalters*—Stuttgart, 1955, page 81.

today and in what torture also. Unlike believing Christians, or even Jews and pagans, they live without any metaphysical outlook unless perhaps they have fallen into superstition. (This reminds us, once again, of Vilmar's comments.) Their orientation is exclusively and incontestably toward temporal concerns, and in this respect seven times more so than the Jews or pagans, having again fallen into the slavery of sin, death and the devil. And yet they do not become really aware of their state of subjection and their diabolically caused disintegration, for the false guides of individualism, rationalism and modern views of society, ruining the spirit of man, keep them in bondage. They are quite conscious of the increasing chaos in all areas of human life, and they also make attempts to correct particular errors in the scientific and socio-political concepts of our time when these are especially notorious. But they find that they are inadequate to utilize the new range of thought and the increase of technical and intellectual means for world conquest, for the purposes of a satisfying development of personality. In all of this they try only to discover a defense against death and chaos, and consequently, as if they were mentally ill, they no longer possess any access to the spiritual world of Christian redemption. Moreover, their standards for "right" and "wrong" become confused with "usefulness" and "harmfulness." Their reason and their ability to perceive have been weakened to such an extent that an unbridgeable gulf exists between intellect and will power, as between feeling and instinct.

This disintegration of the individual consequently forms the visible aspect of society also, for social groups can only be representative of the individual's understanding of life and his attitude toward life. That is why societies also are increasingly assuming the character of demoniacal creatures of compulsion. Perhaps enough has been said to indicate that a general examination of the ways and means of obtaining Christ's salvation, as they are presently established among us in their apparently unshakable and "Protestant" form, is a divine command at this time.

II

This courage in facing the situation realistically is growing in scope just as the need for the Mother Church's spirituality is being realized again, and life *with her* and *from her* is desired once more. In Barmen this all occurred in the name of the German Evangelical Church. Barmen was consequently the completion of a turning toward universal Christian truths which would have caused a rousing "Protestant" expression of indignation if they had been proposed at a conference of German Evangelical pastors during the previous century. A knowledge of these truths puts an end to what was known and disseminated as "reformed knowledge of the gospel" within popular Protestantism, and prior to the Synod in Barmen. This included the idea of direct access to the presence of God, the distinction of the visible from the invisible Church (the principal endeavor of God's enemies until now has been to force Christians into a contemplative refuge of inward subjectivity,) the bringing of Church order into accord with secular principles and the assigning of this order's authority to secular courts, the termination of the teaching order and the dilution of doctrine, the denial of all binding authority of dogma, and other points which could be mentioned here. The risk of an excommunication by a "State Bishop" was then called a symptom of the "ecclesiastical development" which was beginning to be apparent in the Evangelical world, but even then it soon became evident that there was considerable hesitation in proceeding further along this path. Even to a greater extent it is now being recognized in the dominant outlook of most Protestants, including both the layfolk as well as their pastors, that it is still a question of belonging to that group which understood the gospel according to those reformers called Evangelical.

However, theology of this kind is wholly unable to redeem modern man from his subjection and to transmit to him the divine powers that would enable him to pierce the armor that surrounds him. This is the predicament of mankind at a time in the history of the world and of salvation when all of us are awaiting the one, re-united Church, the unity of brotherly love, together with unity in the knowledge and ministration of the divine means of salvation and in the order of the Church's ministry (Eph. 4), helping to lead all men of good will out of darkness into the light. We shall try to set forth an idea of this expected help from the Church in seven principal points:

1. Man is a unity of body, soul and spirit. He misjudges and destroys himself in thinking that he is merely a "rational being" or if he tries to understand or overcome his vital problems in an individualistic or collectivistic way. Furthermore, whether he knows it or not, he is always a member of a "corpus"—either the "corpus" of the first or the second Adam, in the words of Paul (I Cor. 15). Along with this, he is also always a participant in the forming of history who also endures its effects while engaged in shaping it. However, in our time, people as we meet them daily in our churches are really sick, for they imagine that they can live under obligation to the body only, or to the

soul or the spirit alone. They boast of their supposed freedom, individualistically misunderstood, and at the same time lose themselves in the anonymity of the masses. They express only scorn for their own history and repudiate any responsibility for the future.

The Church confronts these sick people with the "Word." But with *which Word* really? Is it "the one Word of God, which *is* Jesus Christ as He is revealed through the testimony of Holy Scripture" (Thesis I of the Barmen Declaration), or is it instead the "spoken and written Word" about Jesus Christ? There should properly be no such contrast, but in practice the contrast does exist in the Church. For if we ask a Church member (or even a pastor) what is meant by the expression *"Word of God,"* we receive almost always the reply that it is exclusively the "spoken and written Word" of the Bible which is meant, and specifically in accordance with the interpretation which humanism and enlightenment have given to the terms *"Word"* and *"Word of God."* But will "words" help and heal men? Quite apart from the question concerning the provision of the "Word of God" for Christian people during the fifteen hundred years that preceded the invention of printing, man is now actually unable, without assistance, to understand the text of the printed Bible whether in seeing or hearing it (and particularly in these days of superficial reading material). It is also a fact that man can receive and digest central biblical concepts such as freedom, righteousness, faith and sacrifice, and others also, only by means of spiritual antennae which he uses in a natural way as a member of a secularized world. With such a rationalized "Word of God," emptied of its Christian content, man in his present disintegration and in his subjection to a false attitude toward life, cannot be brought to a stop or saved. This is why there is so often a despairing and weary resignation among our best Christians in view of the apparently invulnerable fortress of the "hardened" world, whereas a return to the *whole* word of God, which is the living person and living work of the incarnate Son of God, offers every possibility of reaching our fellow-men even when the pure "spoken and written Word" no longer reaches them at all!

2. This dry, intellectualizing of the Christian phenomenon, "the Word of God," can be demonstrated in a particularly striking way when we compare how differently modern man and the men of the New Testament (and of the entire Bible) interpret the concept *"to understand."* We think of it primarily as a function of the mind and thus try to work out with the mind and for the mind "the knowledge of Jesus Christ" and His salvation, while the New Testament considers understanding as a process which involves the whole man with his entire strength of mind, will, soul and body. In the New Testament, *knowledge* means that man surrenders himself with love and sacrifices himself, and therefore he "knows even as he is known," primarily as God knows him. The decadent totalitarian systems have generally recognized this phenomenon, and have taken advantage of it, far more consistently than the Church.

It is a liberating experience for modern man to learn from the New Testament that the "preaching of the gospel" which leads to knowledge is not so much an exposition but rather a "proclamation of God's kingdom" through the divine action of liturgy, sermon and sacrament, and that the Lord did not merely commission His apostles to "preach" but sent them "to seek, to feed, and through His priestly sacrifice to reconcile men with God";

he learns moreover that the authorized ministers of Christ shall "forgive and retain" the sins of the baptized, and that all believers are to be guided by the "bearers of the keys"; and that intercession and excommunication are spiritual means to ensure the effective activity of the kingdom of God (I Cor. 5:5). It is for this reason that man's salvation requires "fishers of men," and pastors, priests, and bearers of reconciling power, to exercise authority, as well as preachers, but not because this is the best way to approach people, as man might suppose, but rather because the Lord does not will the transmission of salvation in any other way. All of this proceeds from His loving, pastoral wisdom, for it is only in this way that man can participate in divine salvation in its fullness.

All of those who are authorized by the Lord to fish for men, and to feed and guide them, have no qualifications of their own to offer (II Cor. 3:5), but they work *in Christ's stead* (see the statement concerning the practical work of the Confessional Synod of the German Evangelical Church, at Barmen). If, however, frightened by the possibility that such authority may be abused (Mt. 20:24-28), the Church arbitrarily and faint-heartedly abridges and reduces the multiplicity of these tasks and authorities (providing, for instance, nothing more than an enlightening sermon), the people are then necessarily receiving salvation in an insufficient manner and are consequently being abandoned to spiritual starvation and demoralization.

3. If we wish to perceive this situation more clearly, we must keep in mind that man can only be understood in the light of certain assumptions. There are no men who are wholly free of some kind of *"guidance,"* and if the Church does not lay claim to the tasks and authorities

we have mentioned, there will immediately be other "pastors, fishers of men, reconcilers, priests and preachers" to take her place. The physician becomes a "spiritual adviser." Nature, art and hobbies become subjects for meditation. The performance of ordinary duties becomes the "service of God." Martyrdom and sacrifice are replaced by world betterment. Consequently it was an act of liberation when God allowed the pastors to be tempted during the recent struggles between Church and State, when the enemy wished to attack and destroy the entire flock. At that time, whatever was said by our reformed brethren concerning the sacred character of ordination, and what the fourth thesis of the Barmen Declaration affirmed, and whatever else, since that time, has contributed to a better knowledge and understanding of the ministry, especially in the Lutheran Churches, is not only in revolutionary contrast to what was commonly taught regarding the ministry before 1934, and to what was practiced also, but it has likewise considerably increased the general effectiveness of the laity. When the ministry is exercised with the fullness of the tasks and abilities with which our Lord endows His servants, it becomes independent of the natural peculiarities, special talents or personal failings of the minister, but also gives both the pastor and the flock the assurance that Christ's authority can be exercised with good conscience, and this point is also being proclaimed and practised by those who represent the so-called *Gemeinde Prinzips* but only with much self-defense and a continual burdening of the individual Church member. That is the reason for the questions concerning the proper legitimation of those commissioned by Christ as fishers of men, pastors, reconcilers, preachers and bishops, and for inquiries regarding the coordination and subordination of the various offices themselves, subject to the office of leadership (vested in a president, bishop, primate or the chairman of a council, etc.). These are questions of the greatest importance in our missionary work among the people. If we answer these questions with greater clarity and courtesy, there will be less possibility of any misuse of an office in the sense of self-glorification of the office-holder (in the Church's struggles of our day the people of God in both the local congregations and the Church as a whole, have become wide awake!). The faithful too will be freer to assume tasks in the service of God according to the order of the "universal priesthood." The innermost secret of the pastoral ministry, including the very highest pastoral office of all, is the "loosing and binding." For this is always a pastoral, and never a synodal procedure. Properly understood however, it is simultaneously the strongest check against centralism in the whole order of the Church. For the limitation of the pastor, by restricting his ministry to the "loosing and binding," actually requires that the pattern of the corporate life of the congregation as well as the whole Church generally, functioning through the synod (i.e., through the work undertaken together by both the lay workers and the pastors) must be fully regulated. The Evangelical reader, who at this point is unable to rid himself of customary Protestant anxieties, should at least permit Leslie Newbigin, a bishop of the united Church of South India, and a leading theologian of the Ecumenical Movement, to explain the importance of the transmission of ministerial authority "in orderly succession from generation to generation" and how it affects the spirit and the task of the Church when this continuity (i.e., this succession) is broken by schisms within the Church and divides into diverging lines.[2] Loving concern, of course, recurrently revives the Church's endeavor to find the best method for awakening men to faith in Christ. Nevertheless, we are forbidden to underestimate the importance of asking whether this very endeavor is being carried out in accordance with the standard established by the Lord of the Church.

4. We are all aware of the modern yearning for the experience of true *Confession*. This is not a yearning for mere "peace of mind" or "deceptive illusion" which would not be permissible for Christians, but is quite simply a matter of an authentic, spiritual longing for the experience of *forgiveness,* and for pastoral guidance in the paths of God, and for an increase of joy in the kingdom of heaven. (Our Lord did not reject the rational questioning by Nathanael, nor did He consider the yearning of shepherdless sheep for a loving shepherd, or the compelling plea of the sinful woman for compassionate mercy, or that of Zacchaeus either, as an "unjustified desire for security" but rather as something to be acknowledged and granted, and rightly so.)

Since sin is not only a personal matter between God and the individual sinner, but is also a violation and destruction of the Church as the Body of Christ, the confession of sins and removal of guilt are therefore much more than just a personal exoneration of the individual; they are actually an act of divine judgment and an increase of the glory of Christ's Body in this world. In this respect the field is ripe for the harvest indeed!

5. Wherever *Confession* in this sense is being practiced, man enters into a new personal relationship to his own

2 Leslie Newbigin: *Von der Spaltung zur Einheit,* Ev. Missionsverlag, Stuttgart, 1956, page 104.

history and even to history in general. Modern man is rightly inclined to distrust all idealisms. He has seen through the farce of abstract demands and goals. He is therefore virtually prepared for the divine encouragement that he ought to be saved, not in spite of his sins but because of them, and that his life is precious, not through disregard for his trespasses, but rather because he is a "saint" if he can remain aware of his sinful existence, but in such a way that the seal of forgiveness and the outpouring of the Holy Spirit will rest upon his sinfulness: the former things have passed away; behold, they are made new! (II Cor. 5:17). There also develops a new faith in the history of the *Visible Church,* in that history which, from the self-sacrifice of the apostles (apparent on almost every page of the gospels) to the self-denial of the pastors and congregations of this present day, appears so greatly burdened and yet is permeated with such glory of grace and life.

6. Such a view of history and the Church opens the way to *freedom*—for men whose longing for freedom is beyond telling. For there is real freedom from sin and death and the devil for anyone who obediently unites with, and submits to the "free kingdom" of the Body of Christ which is the Church of God. True freedom does not mean escape into loneliness, "away from all others," for we can never become truly free of them. Our freedom opens up to us after our liberation from a condition of fear, liberating us toward *"nearness to our neighbor,"* and making us free in Christ from the wrath of God. Are we willing to help the faithful of our Churches toward that inner freedom and joy which always was, or ought to be, the strength of the Church at all times? Our willingness should be shown by our permitting the careful study and consideration of our Protestant ecclesiastical organization to determine

whether it is established and operative in a manner pleasing to God within the visible Body of Christ, which, in union with our Lord, the Head of the Body in heaven, has existed in this present world since the outpouring of the Holy Spirit. A fearful refusal of such an inquiry would indicate insecurity, especially when the rightness of the one standard can only be maintained by distorting the position taken by another Church, particularly in opposing her fundamental principles by pointing out her *apparent* errors and by arousing the so-called *"anti-*complexes" of Evangelical Christians. An attitude of this kind among individual members of the ministry, or of corporate groups or others having influence and authority, will only deprive our Church people of their spiritual joy. On the other hand, a sincere willingness to allow an inquiry of this kind presents all the possibilities, otherwise beyond reach, for a charitable questioning of the other Church in regard to anything contestable in her belief and practice, and likewise the chance *to be heard.* And since the Church is the mother of our spiritual life, it can be expected that through such meeting of separated Christians, relations between men will likewise become better.

7. We find ourselves in the midst of the problems arising from the ordinary behavior of our fellow-men today. If we can again establish a customary and human *ethics* based upon the sacrifice of Christ, and developing from it, and acknowledge and take hold of the Holy Spirit as the lawgiver of the New Covenant, and be zealous for recognition of the biblical doctrine concerning the reward of good works, then the ordinary, daily life of man would be accorded an entirely new dignity as the realm of a participation of *love,* regardless of the ups and downs of secular history or its ways of life. Resignation and the

sense of inferiority would disappear, but there would be a growth of joy in life.

We can only make brief allusions to the opportunities that are offered in our time for the awakening of new spiritual life in the fellowship of the Church when there is a willingness to return to the lost or weakened Catholic and Apostolic truths in their integrity. The new beginning which was made at Barmen in 1934 through God's grace, within our Evangelical communion, must mature into the full life of the holy Church as the universal Christian credo confesses it. In Ephesians 4:1-16 and in John 17, we will find reason for a sure and certain confidence that God will not withhold His blessing and help for such an endeavor.